AMERICAN HISTORY

VOLUME VIII:

WASHINGTON

JACOB ABBOTT

SANDYCROFT PUBLISHING

American History Vol. VIII: Washington

By Jacob Abbott

First published 1865

This edition ©2017

Sandycroft Publishing

http://sandycroftpublishing.com

CONTENTS

PREFACE..i

CHAPTER I
Early Days

The Five Periods of Washington's Life.—Birthplace of Washington.—The Mother of Washington.—His School.—Washington's Brother Lawrence.—The Estate at Mount Vernon.—The Fairfax Family.—Washington's Connection with the Fairfax Family.—General Geographical Features of Virginia.—The Lands of Lord Fairfax.—Organization of an Exploring and Surveying Party.—The Surveying Party.—Description of the Map.—Various Adventures.—Mode of Living.—Greenway Court..1

CHAPTER II
The Valley of the Ohio

Situation of the Valley.—Value of This Western Territory.—Conflicting Claims of the French and of the English to the Possession of the Valley.—Merits of the Question.—Rights of the Indians.—Advantageous Position of the French in Entering into the Contest.—Disadvantages of the English Situation.—Formation of the Ohio Company.—Employment of Washington by the Ohio Company.—Appointment of George Washington to a Military Command.—His Military Studies.—Death of Lawrence Washington.—Mount Vernon.—Preparations for War.—Reluctance of the People of the Colony to Undertake the War.—The Cooperation of the Other Atlantic Colonies Obtained.—Interference of Jurisdiction and Authority during the War.—Difficulties of Being at the Same Time Many and One.—General Course and Result of the War.—The Part Performed by Washington.—Nature of His Services.—Occasion of the First Battle and Victory.—Advance to the Attack.—Return of Washington to Private Life..12

CHAPTER III
LIFE AT MOUNT VERNON

The Young Widow.—Crossing the Ferry.—Mrs. Custis.—The Acquaintance Agreeable.—The White House.—Washington Elected a Member of the Legislature.—Washington's Aversion to Public Speaking and to Occasions of Parade and Display.—The Marriage.—Establishment at Mount Vernon.—Plantation Life.—System of Commercial Exchange.—Practical Inconveniences of the System.—Specimens of the Correspondence.—The Estate at Mount Vernon.—Horses and Carriages.—Dogs and Hunting.—Fishing.—Busy Life.—Daily Routine at Mount Vernon.—Visits and Company.—Belvoir.—Visits to Annapolis.—Public Duties.—Plan for Reclaiming the Dismal Swamp.—Exploration of the Swamp.—Expedition to the Valley of the Ohio.—Adventures in the Valley.—Voyage down the River.—Danger.—Duration of the Period of Quiet Life at Mount Vernon.—Movements that Preceded the Revolution.—Meeting of the First Continental Congress.—Appointment of Commander-in-Chief.—Farewell to Mount Vernon..28

CHAPTER IV
THE REVOLUTION

Qualities Necessary in a Commander-in-Chief.—Incipient Difficulties.—Conflicts of Authority.—Mrs. Washington's Visit.—Mount Vernon in Danger.—Arrival of Mrs. Washington at Cambridge.—Influence of Mrs. Washington in Camp.—Calls for Help and Protection from the Coast.—Insubordination and Unmanageableness of the Men.—No Ammunition.—Necessity of Remedying These Evils without Making Them Known.—Washington Almost in Despair.—Discontent and Dissatisfaction of the People.—Final Triumph of the Army before Boston.—The Contest for the Possession of New York.—Washington Is Overpowered by the Difficulties of His Situation.—A Party Beginning to be Formed against Him.—The People not to be too Severely Censured for Their Doubts And Misgivings.—The Character of Washington Retrieved.—Character and Motives of Washington's Enemies.—The Third Dark Period of the Revolution.—The Opposition Revived.—Such an Opposition Unavoidable.—Measures Resorted to by the Party

Opposed to Washington.—General Gates.—General Conway.—End of General Conway.—Conway's Letter...47

CHAPTER V
Negotiations for Peace

Chronology.—Complicated Nature of the Negotiations.—Implication of Other Governments in the Quarrel.—The Case of Holland.—Henry Laurens.—Capture of Laurens.—He Remains Faithful and Firm.—The Capture of the Papers Leads to War between England and Holland.—Various Complications.—Party Conflicts in Congress in Respect to the Appointment of Commissioners.—The Commissioners.—Benjamin Franklin.—Complications and Difficulties on the British Side.—The Question in Parliament.—Effect of the Surrender of Cornwallis.—An Alternative Still Presented.—Attempt to Separate America from France.—Attempt to Negotiate with Washington and Congress.—The Three Essentials.—Technicalities and Points of Etiquette.—True Character of the French Intervention.—Interference of French and American.—Interests in the Question of Peace.—The Western Boundary.—The Fisheries.—Diplomacy.—Claims of Compensation for the American Loyalists.—Terms of the Treaty Finally Agreed Upon.—Long Protraction of the Negotiations.—Final Withdrawal of the British Army......................65

CHAPTER VI
The Disbanding of the Army

Resignation of Washington.—The Nature of the Greatness of Washington.—Assumptions of Other Founders of Empire.—The Soldiers.—The Revolt in 1781.—Causes of the Revolt.—Why Congress Could not Act Effectually.—The Crisis.—Danger and Difficulty of the Situation.—Washington's Danger.—Endeavor of the British to Take Advantage of the Difficulty.—Measures Adopted by Washington.—The Mutineers Come to a Stand at Princeton.—Opening of the Conferences.—Delegation from Congress.—The Emissaries from the British Army.—President Reed and the Delegation.—The Conference.—The British Agents.—Rewards Offered for the Apprehension of the Spies.—Just Estimation of the Conduct of the Mutineers.—General Discontent of the Army toward the Close of the War.—General Washington's Remonstrances.—Some Small Excuse for the Injustice.—The Proper Remedy.—Special Exertions Made by Washington to Avert the Danger.—Furloughs.—Threatened Conspiracy among the Troops.—Anonymous Addresses Circulated in Camp.—Conduct of Washington in the Emergency.—Washington's Farewell to the Army.—Washington's Parting with His Officers.—Settlement of the Accounts.—Final Resignation.—The Ceremony.—Return to Mount Vernon...82

CHAPTER VII
The Confederation

Three Successive Forms of Combination Adopted by the States.—Essential Difference in the Nature of These Systems.—Nature of a Confederation.—The Union.—Duration of the Continental Congress.—First Movement in Favor of a Confederation.—Debates on the Subject in the Continental Congress.—Articles of Confederation Adopted and Proposed to the States.—Provisions of the Proposed Confederation.—Majority Required.—The States Equal under the Confederation.—No Executive Department.—Common Citizenship.—Restrictions on Separate State Sovereignty.—Provision for the Settlement of Questions of Controversy Arising between One State and Another.—The Articles of Confederation Adopted by Congress and Transmitted to the States.—Little Advantage Gained.—Influence of Peace and War in Respect to the Operation of the American System of Government.—Termination of the Revolutionary War.—Resignation of the Secretary of the Treasury.—The Army.—State of Completely Suspended Animation Reached at Last.—Subjects Demanding Attention from the General Government during These Times.—General Conviction of the Necessity that a Stronger Government Should be Established.—Shay's Insurrection.—The General Government Powerless.—The Insurrection Subdued.—All Confidence in the Confederate Government Finally Lost..103

CHAPTER VIII
The Union

Origin of the Convention.—Difficulties in the Way.—Great Importance Attached to the Idea of State Sovereignty.—General

Character of the Convention.—Injunction of Secrecy.—Jealousy of State Rights and State Sovereignty.—Political Conservatism.—The Question of Aristocracy and Democracy.—Diversities of Opinion in Respect to Details.—Parties.—The Large and Small States.—Free and Slave States.—Navigation Laws.—Wise Counsels Prevail in the End.—The Two Compromises.—General Features of the System that was Adopted.—Surrender of Power by the States.—The Judicial Department.—The Plan Submitted to the Confederate Congress.—The Ratification.—Election of President..118

CHAPTER IX
Inauguration of the Government

Departure of Washington from Mount Vernon.—Escort of Neighbors and Friends.—Washington's Reply.—Progress of the Journey.—Universal Enthusiasm.—Celebration at the Bridge at Trenton.—Arrival at New York.—Entrance into New York.—The Barges.—The Landing.—The Procession to the Governor's.—The Inauguration.—Administration of the Oath.—Rejoicings.—Concluding Ceremonies.—Influential Men Associated with Washington in the Government.—John Adams.—Alexander Hamilton.—The Federalist.—Hamilton's Public Career.—His Untimely End.—The Fundamental Question of Politics.—Opinions of Adams and Hamilton.—A Monarchy Impossible.—Opinions of Jefferson and Madison.—Equal Political Rights for All Men the Only Safe Policy of Government.—The Only Just as Well as the Only Safe Policy.—The Right of Suffrage the Safeguard of the Poor.—Position of Jefferson in Washington's Government.—James Madison.—Incipient Divergency of Political Opinion.—The First Test Question.—Adams's Opinion.—Hamilton.—Jefferson.—Gradual Formation of the Great Federal and Democratic Parties..132

CHAPTER X
Working of the System

Soon Put to the Test.—The Anglo-Saxon Principle of Government.—This Principle Acknowledged and Acted upon by the English People.—Different Modes of Ascertaining the National Will.—The Consent of the Governed.—Examples in Point.—The General Government of the United States.—The General and the Local Interests Requiring a Different Provision.—Fundamental Idea of the General Government.—Question of the Seat of Government.—The City of Washington.—Transfer of the Government to Washington..........156

LIST OF ENGRAVINGS

Portrait of Washington..ii
Map: Early life of Washington..9
Washington's first combat..25
Arrival of Mrs. Washington in camp...50
Franklin and the electrical kite..71
Washington, president elect...137
House of Representatives in session..157

PREFACE

It is the design of this work to narrate, in a clear, simple, and intelligible manner, the leading events connected with the history of our country, from the earliest periods, down, as nearly as practicable, to the present time. The several volumes will be illustrated with all necessary maps and with numerous engravings, and the work is intended to comprise, in a distinct and connected narrative, all that it is essential for the general reader to understand in respect to the subject of it, while for those who have time for more extended studies, it may serve as an introduction to other and more copious sources of information.

The author hopes also that the work may be found useful to the young, in awakening in their minds an interest in the history of their country and a desire for further instruction in respect to it. While it is doubtless true that such a subject can be really grasped only by minds in some degree mature, still the author believes that many young persons, especially such as are intelligent and thoughtful in disposition and character, may derive both entertainment and instruction from a perusal of these pages.

I have been greatly assisted in the preparation of the concluding volumes of this series by the vast stores of information in respect to the history of the American Revolution collected with so much industry, and arranged and illustrated with so much accuracy, taste, and skill, by Lossing, in his *Field-Book of the Revolution*. For felicity of description, copiousness and interest of detail, philosophic clearness of narration, and graphic power of delineation, both with pencil and pen, in picturing the scenes and incidents described, it stands at the head of works on the history of this country, and forms an inexhaustible treasury of useful and entertaining information in respect to the events, the actors, and the scenes, of revolutionary history, equally attractive to old and young.

WASHINGTON

CHAPTER I
EARLY DAYS

THE FIVE PERIODS OF WASHINGTON'S LIFE

The life of George Washington, to which the remarkable succession of striking scenes and incidents which it presents, impart, in general, an extremely picturesque and dramatic character, resembled the dramas of the poets in this additional particular, namely, that it naturally divides itself into five quite distinct, and in some respects strongly contrasted, portions as follows.

1. The years of his childhood and youth.
2. His first public career as a civil and military officer in the service of the British and colonial authorities against the French and Indians in the valley of the Ohio.
3. A period of eighteen years of private life spent on his estate at Mount Vernon.
4. His military career during the war of the revolution.
5. The period of his civil services in the work of organizing and administering the government of the United States under the federal constitution.

It is with this last portion of the history of Washington that we have most to do in this volume—considered as a continuation of the narrative of American History, which was brought by the last volume to the close of the war of the revolution. In order however to understand and appreciate the course which Washington pursued in the last great act of the drama, we must consider somewhat particularly the previous portions of his life, with a view of tracing the course of experience, discipline, and trial by which he was prepared to pursue the line of action at the end of his career, which has given him the very exalted place he occupies in history, and made him the admiration of mankind.

Birthplace of Washington

George Washington lived, in his early childhood, with his father and mother and brothers and sisters, in an old fashioned Virginia farmhouse on the banks of the Potomac not far from its mouth. The house had a roof sloping behind almost down to the ground, and the chimneys were built outside of it—one at each end, against the wall, according to the fashion which then prevailed in Virginia. The building was old at the time of Washington's birth, and has long since entirely disappeared. A descendant of the family has however placed a large stone tablet upon the spot, which is marked with this inscription:

> Here,
> The 11th of February, 1732,
> GEORGE WASHINGTON
> Was Born.

The Mother of Washington

The Washington family removed from the house near the mouth of the Potomac where Washington was born, while he was yet a mere child, and went to live in another very similar house near the town of Fredericksburg. There, before many years, his father died, and Washington was left almost under the sole charge of his mother. She was a most excellent woman, and devoted all her time to the care and instruction of her children. She took the utmost pains to instill into their minds the principles of virtue, and to train them to habits of industry, punctuality, and scrupulous faithfulness in the performance of every duty. It was to the training that this most excellent mother gave to her son that the full development of those exalted qualities of mind and heart which subsequently gave him so vast an ascendancy over the minds of his countrymen, was in a great measure due.

His School

The school which George attended when he was a boy, was of a very humble character. It was kept in a small country schoolhouse by the wayside, not far from his mother's house. The teacher was the sexton of the parish. His name was Hobby. At this school Washington learned thee elementary branches of education—reading, writing, arithmetic, and accounts. His mother devoted a great deal of attention to him in respect to the preparation of his lessons, and trained him to the habit of taking great pains with everything that he did, of fulfilling every allotted task to the very best of his ability, and of never allowing himself to carry in to his teacher any careless, hasty, or ill-executed work. So well indeed was his work done at this time that he and his mother felt an interest in preserving many of his books of school exercises, on account of their very neat and correct appearance; and they have been kept to this day, and are now shown to visitors at Mount Vernon, among other mementos and souvenirs of the great statesman's life.

Washington's Brother Lawrence

The oldest of George's brothers was named Lawrence. He was strictly speaking only a half brother, as he was born during a previous marriage. He was also fourteen or fifteen years older than George, and so was never by any means a companion or playmate for him. Thus the relation that he sustained to George was more like that of an uncle than of a brother. He was however very fond of George and took great interest in his welfare. Being the oldest son, he was considered, according to the English ideas which then prevailed, as in some sense the head of the family, and was sent to England to be educated.

He returned from England when George was about seven or eight years old, and immediately formed a strong attachment to his little brother, and ever afterward, as long as he lived, took a great interest in him.

The Estate at Mount Vernon

Not long after Lawrence Washington returned to Virginia, he joined the English army and went to the West Indies, where a war was raging between England and Spain. The commanding officer of the squadron in which he served was Admiral Vernon, and Lawrence seems to have become strongly attached to him. The war did not continue long, and when peace was made Lawrence Washington returned to Virginia, to his brother George's great joy. He established himself upon an estate which he possessed on the banks of the Potomac, and named the place Mount Vernon, in honor of Admiral Vernon, the English officer under whom he had served in the West Indies.

This estate ultimately descended to his brother, the hero of this narrative, and has since become world renowned, and specially sacred in the minds of all Americans, as the home during his life and the place of sepulture after his death, of the father of his country.

Very soon after his establishment at Mount Vernon Lawrence Washington was married to Miss Anne Fairfax, the daughter of Sir William Fairfax, an English gentleman of wealth and high station, who resided upon an estate named Belvoir, which was situated on the banks of the Potomac some miles below Mount Vernon.[1]

The Fairfax Family

Sir William Fairfax was the cousin of Lord Fairfax, an English nobleman, who had inherited an immense tract of land in Virginia which had been some years previously granted to his ancestors by the crown.

---

[1] The place was so named from Belvoir Castle, one of the most celebrated ancient castles of England, and one of the most magnificent at the present day. It is the residence of the Duke of Rutland, and is situated in the eastern part of the island on the confines of Lincolnshire. The name—originally a French one, given to the vale which the castle overlooks, and to the castle itself, by William the Conqueror, or by his Norman followers—has been anglicized in pronunciation, in modern times, into Beevor Castle, and Beevor Vale.

About the time of the marriage of Miss Anne Fairfax to Mr. Lawrence Washington, Lord Fairfax came himself to America to visit his estates. He was entirely at liberty to roam over the world as he pleased, being possessed of a large fortune and having no family. Indeed he was somewhat uneasy and discontented in England from the effect of a bitter disappointment in love which he had met with when a young man. On his arrival in Virginia he was greatly impressed with the magnificence of the country in general, and the grandeur of his own domains, which included a vast tract of charming ground lying between the rivers Potomac and Rappahannock. He took up his residence for a time at Belvoir, with his cousin Sir William, where he supplied himself with horses, dogs, and handsome equipages, in the English style, and devoted himself to fishing, hunting and the other athletic sports of which English country gentlemen are so fond.

Washington's Connection with the Fairfax Family

George Washington, who at this time resided frequently at his brother Lawrence's at Mount Vernon, was of course a frequent visitor at Belvoir, where both Lord Fairfax and Sir William became well acquainted with him, and he soon began to be quite a favorite with them, as it seems he was, even in those early days, with all who knew him. He used to accompany the gentlemen on their hunting expeditions, and often rendered them great service by his intimate knowledge of the country, and by the fertility of his resources in the various emergencies and exigencies of life in the woods. Although yet quite young, being at this time only about fifteen or sixteen years of age, he was well grown and strong. He was an excellent rider. He could easily manage any horse they gave him, and he galloped on after the game, over the most difficult and rugged ground, with so much courage and skill as greatly to please his older companions.

With all this he was extremely careful and considerate—he took no useless risks, and evinced in his whole conduct and demeanor a degree of calmness and deliberation in all difficult and trying emergencies, and a soundness of judgment, above his years. Lord Fairfax became greatly interested in the young man, and strongly attached to him.

General Geographical Features of Virginia

By carefully examining any map of Virginia with reference to the mountain chains and the flow of the rivers, the reader will observe that there are two ranges of mountains, or rather of mountainous country, extending from northeast to southwest in the interior of the state, and a wide valley between them. This valley is called the valley of the Shenandoah, from the river of that name which flows through it. This valley opens to the northward, where the Shenandoah empties into the Potomac.

The mountains on the east side of this valley are those of the Blue Ridge, while the west side of it is bounded by the ranges of the Allegheny Mountains.

To the eastward of Blue Ridge the land slopes and the rivers flow toward the Atlantic Ocean, and to the west of the Allegheny Mountains the slope is toward the valley of the Ohio.

Thus the territory of Virginia consists of an eastern slope of land inclining toward the sea, a western one descending into the valleys of the Ohio and the Mississippi, and a great valley between them, opening toward the north and carrying its waters by the river Shenandoah into the Potomac.

The Lands of Lord Fairfax

Almost all the settlements which existed in Virginia, in Washington's early days, were on the eastern slope. The western slope was almost entirely in the possession of the Indians. Even the valley of the Shenandoah between them was very little inhabited by white men, although various adventurers and backwoodsmen had found their way into it—some to trade with the Indians for furs, others to find fertile lands where they could settle and make their farms without having any purchase-money to pay. The log huts of these people were scattered here and there over the territory, in openings which they had made in the woods, and there were roving bands of Indians, also, who roamed about by the paths which they had made through the forests, or paddled up and down the rivers in their birch canoes.

The vast tract of land which Lord Fairfax claimed extended beyond the Blue Ridge into this valley, but the portion beyond the mountains had never been surveyed, and had been very imperfectly explored. In the meantime, as has already been said, roving adventurers were beginning to go in and establish themselves in the country, choosing of course the choicest sites, and it was to be feared that if they were allowed to continue their illegal possession too long, they might claim a right to the property, and it might become very difficult in the end either to compel them to pay the price for the land which they occupied, or to eject them from it.

Organization of an Exploring and Surveying Party

Under these circumstances Lord Fairfax proposed to young Washington the plan of organizing an exploring party to proceed into the Shenandoah Valley, there to survey and take possession of the lands belonging to him, with a view to the formal assertion of his rights as owner of the property, and to prepare the way for regular sales of the lands to future settlers. Washington readily undertook the work. He was admirably well qualified for it. He had taken great interest in studying the science and art of surveying, and the inspection of some of the field-books which he had kept made so strong an impression upon Lord Fairfax's mind, and gave him so high an idea of his young friend's science and skill as to satisfy him that he was well qualified for the work which he proposed.

Young Washington, though still only fifteen or sixteen years of age, was of an athletic and vigorous frame. He was accustomed to life in the woods. He was prudent, grave, and cautious in his conduct to a degree entirely beyond his years. The plan was accordingly decided upon, and the arrangements were at once made for carrying it into effect. Washington was to receive about fifteen dollars a day for his services during the time that he should be gone.

The Surveying Party

Young Washington had one companion on this expedition in the person of George William Fairfax, the son of Sir William. He was a few years older than Washington himself. In addition to these two the party comprised some attendants. Others were to be obtained in the country to he surveyed. A considerable number of followers and assistants are always required on such expeditions as these.

Besides the necessity of a company for the purpose of mutual aid and protection in a journey through so wild and lawless a country, the simple business of running a line with compass and chain through the woods requires a party of several men to carry it forward promptly and with despatch. There must be two chainmen, one for each end of the chain—and a compass man to carry the compass, and to set it, when it is required to regulate the direction of the line run—and two or three axe men, to go forward and clear the way when necessary, and also to fell trees across small streams to serve as bridges for the party to pass over. The surveyor himself cannot perform any of these duties, for he must carry the field-book, and must be incessantly employed in making notes in it of the distances run, the streams crossed, the quality of the land, the character of the timber, the situation of waterfalls where mills might be built, and other such particulars.

Besides the number of persons actually employed in the process of surveying, there are others necessary to carry the provisions required for the party, or the guns and ammunition for procuring food from the forest.

It is not to be supposed however that Washington took all this force with him, from Mount Vernon and Belvoir. He relied in a great measure for these purposes on the aid that he could obtain in the valley itself from the settlers, and from the Indians, whom it was necessary sometimes to employ as guides.

Description of the Map

The adjoining map shows the situation of the Shenandoah Valley in reference to the eastern slope of the territory of Virginia. It also shows the position of Mount Vernon, and of the Fairfax residence of Belvoir just below it on the banks of the Potomac. The letter W marks the point on the banks of the river where the city of Washington was afterward built. Farther down the river, and pretty near the mouth of

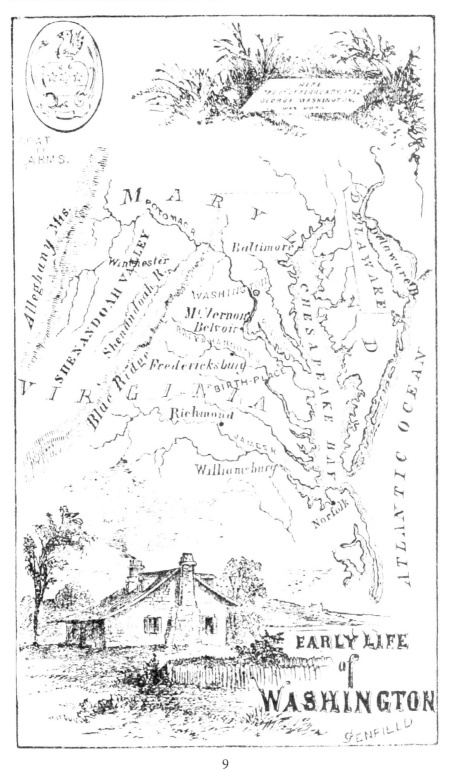

it, the reader will see that the birthplace of Washington is indicated, and also, in the interior, the town of Fredericksburg, near which he lived a long time with his mother, after his father's death, and where he went to school to Master Hobby.

Various Adventures

It was in the month of March that this exploring tour was commenced. It occupied a period of several weeks, at the end of which time the party returned. Washington encountered a great variety of experiences and adventures during his absence, but he accomplished the purpose of his mission in a very satisfactory manner.

Sometimes he and his companion found a lodging for the night in the hut of a settler, though even in these cases, instead of occupying a bed, they usually lay down at night upon blankets, bearskins or straw, with the members of the family—men, women, and children, and perhaps other strangers—bestowed in a similar manner all around them, the forms of the sleepers under their rude coverings revealed by the flickering light of the fire.

They met occasionally with companies of Indians, and at one time they encountered a party of thirty warriors returning from some expedition, bearing a scalp for a trophy. These Indians at their encampment cleared a space of ground, built a fire in the center, and sat around the fire in a circle, and there, to entertain Washington and his companions, went through with some of the wild ceremonies of savage life, which were intermingled with frightful war-whoops and yells, and hideous dances.

Mode of Living

The party depended for food almost wholly upon the game they could shoot, consisting chiefly of wild turkeys and other birds. Provided with supplies of such food as this, they gathered round their camp-fire at night and prepared their suppers, each one cooking for himself his own portion by means of a forked stick with which the strip of flesh was held before the glowing embers of the fire.

Greenway Court

Lord Fairfax was much pleased with the report which Washington brought back of the result of his labors, and with the account which he gave of the beauty and richness of the country, and he determined to go into the valley himself and build a residence there. He did in fact afterward select a spot near where the town of Winchester now stands, and he erected some buildings preliminary to the construction of the intended mansion. He put up a suitable house for his servants, and stables for his horses, and kennels for his dogs, and also a small structure apart from the rest, containing a sleeping room for himself, and also an office, in which he transacted business with his tenants and the men in his employ. The name which he gave the place was Greenway Court.

Here he lived for several years, and Washington was a frequent visitor at his "quarters," as he called them, and was employed a great deal in making explorations and surveys of the surrounding country.

The mansion itself, of Greenway Court, which it was at this time the intention of Lord Fairfax to construct, was to be built in the style of English country residences of the highest class; and so magnificent was the scale on which the wealthy nobleman formed his plan that he set apart a tract of land—most fertile and picturesque in its character—of ten thousand acres, to form the domain to be attached to the residence.

The building was, however, never erected. The whole plan shared the fate of the thousand other attempts which have been made from time to time to introduce the ideas and usages of the feudal aristocracies of Europe into the new world. Those ideas and usages are old trunks which have great vitality where they stand, but cannot bear transplantation to another soil.

CHAPTER II
THE VALLEY OF THE OHIO

SITUATION OF THE VALLEY

The valley of the Shenandoah, as has already been explained, lies between the Blue Ridge and the Allegheny mountains; while beyond the Allegheny Mountains the land slopes toward the west, and opens into the great valley of the Ohio. On the hither side of these mountains the waters all flow to the northward and eastward, and find their way ultimately to the Atlantic Ocean. Beyond them the course of the streams is to the westward and southward into the valley of the Ohio, and thence through the vast basin of the Mississippi to the Gulf of Mexico.

VALUE OF THIS WESTERN TERRITORY

The interest which this territory, or rather that portion of it which forms the valley of the Ohio—the only part which in these early times had yet come seriously into question—possessed in the minds of the colonists on the St. Lawrence and on the Atlantic seaboard, arose not so much from its prospective value as a home for European settlers, as from the vast supplies of furs which might at that time be drawn from it. The land was fertile and the forests luxuriant, and they were filled with wild animals of every kind, some of which produced furs which were of great value in Europe. The country was inhabited by roving tribes of Indians, who indeed cleared and cultivated some small patches of land, but who left far the larger portion of the forests undisturbed, except to hunt and trap the animals that inhabited them, as they depended mainly upon the products of the chase for food and clothing. They were extremely skillful in trapping the fur-bearing animals, and they had the art of curing the peltry which they obtained so far as was necessary for its safe transportation to Europe, where the skins were manufactured into the most soft and luxurious furs, and sold at an enormous profit.

The profit was all the greater on account of the very insignificant value of the merchandise given to the Indians in exchange for the skins, which consisted chiefly of glass beads, gaudy colored calicoes, cheap ornaments such as rings, bracelets, chains and the like, and spirituous liquors of inferior quality and of very trifling cost.

Thus the main object for coveting the possession of the valley of the Ohio in the early days of Washington was to gain the control of the fur trade with the Indians that inhabited it.

Conflicting Claims of the French and of the English to the Possession of the Valley

Both the French and English claimed this territory. The ground of the French claim was that they first discovered and explored the river Mississippi, and according to the ideas in respect to discovery and dominion which then prevailed, any power whose subjects first discovered a river became entitled to jurisdiction over all the country drained by the waters of that river.

Now, as is related in a former volume of this series, a French explorer had gone down with a party in a boat, from the French settlements on the western lakes, until he reached the Mississippi, and had descended for some distance along its course. This vested the title to the whole country drained by the river, including the valley of the Ohio as a portion of it, in the French king—subject of course to such rights of occupancy as were possessed by the Indians.

The English on the other hand maintained that in taking possession of any portion of the seacoast of a continent, and establishing colonies thereon, a power became entitled not only to the land actually occupied by them, but to the territory contiguous to it, to an indefinite distance into the interior, and that no other European power could rightfully interfere with them, by penetrating into the interior by circuitous routes, as the French had done, and were attempting to do. In other words, they claimed that each was entitled to all the territory lying directly back of the portion of the seacoast which they respectively possessed, and no more.

MERITS OF THE QUESTION

In a word, the French claimed a right to the land on account of having first discovered the rivers that drained it, and the English on the ground of having first settled the seacoast which fronted it. Of course there was no possibility of settling such a question as this by argument. Nor even if reasoning and argument could have led never so certainly to a solution, would it have made any difference in the result. Here were the pioneer settlements of two of the most ambitious and powerful nations in the world approaching, on different sides, a vast, rich and mainly unoccupied country, one teeming, too, with wealth all ready to be gathered. The only possible way, as human nature is, of settling the question which should seize the prize, was to ascertain by actual trial which was the strongest.

It is true that some time was spent at the outset in arguments and negotiations—but the object of such discussion on each side was only to amuse and occupy the attention of the other until the preparations for the more serious work could be properly made. Each party immediately commenced making their arrangements for advancing into the disputed territory with a military force sufficient to hold it against all attempts of the other to dispossess them.

RIGHTS OF THE INDIANS

It must be admitted in justice to the parties concerned that neither the French nor English absolutely disregarded the claims of the Indians to the land in dispute. They admitted that the Indians had certain rights of occupancy in the country of their forefathers which they were bound to recognize and to provide for in some amicable manner. In respect to their own rights of discovery and first possession—those of the English based on their occupancy of the coast, and those of the French on their discovery of the rivers—all that each power claimed was that its title was good as against all other European powers claiming to make settlements in the new world. The title of the Indians to the land was to be extinguished, so far as it should be necessary to extinguish it, by friendly negotiations with them and treaties.

These negotiations with the Indians, both parties commenced and eagerly prosecuted during the time while they were making their preparations for the great contest with each other. They convened councils of the tribes, and sent commissioners to them with presents of wampum, trinkets, gunpowder, and rum, to buy over the chiefs, and with smooth words and pretenses of disinterested friendship to cajole the people. The English called themselves the Indians' brothers. The French styled the governor of Canada the Indians' father. Each made treaties of a more or less formal character, with different tribes inhabiting the country, under which they put forward claims to this and that district of country, or to the exclusive right of trading at this or that station, and they argued these claims both with the Indians and with one another in a very serious manner.

This was, however, after all mere by-play. The real question, and the only real question at issue, was which of the two powers was to prove strong enough to expel the other from the territory in dispute with bullets, bayonets, and artillery.

Advantageous Position of the French in Entering into the Contest

In the preliminary movements and negotiations which preceded the great conflict of arms by which it was destined that the question was finally to be settled, the French seem to have had greatly the advantage, on account of the situation of the country in dispute in respect to their possessions on the St. Lawrence. The valley of the Ohio was separated from the English settlements by the ranges of the Allegheny Mountains—which could only be traversed by means of a few difficult and dangerous passes. On the other hand the valley was entirely open to access from the region of the St. Lawrence and the lakes, the whole region on that side being level or gently undulating, and being traversed by multitudes of streams navigable for canoes, which greatly facilitated the movements of expeditions of all sorts, and the transportation of supplies. The French, too, were much more successful than the English in cultivating the acquaintance and friendship of the Indians. The country which their settlements occupied was more favorably situated for the fur trade on account of the immense extent to which it could be penetrated by bateaux and canoes, and also to the greater abundance of the fur bearing animals in the country bordering the northern lakes and rivers than in the region occupied by the English colonies on the Atlantic seaboard. The French, too, were more inclined to fraternize with the Indians, to fall in, good-humoredly, with their customs, and to adopt their modes of life. Sometimes a French trader joined the Indian tribes and lived with them for a time altogether, adopting their dress and their mode of life, and learning their language. In other cases persons who had been taken captive and held as prisoners contrived to ingratiate themselves into the favor of their captors, and after living with them a long time, and becoming thoroughly acquainted with their language, their ideas, their customs of war and diplomacy and their modes of life, would finally obtain their release and return to the French settlements, and would afterward render the most important services to their countrymen as interpreters for embassies sent or received, or as a medium of communication in a great variety of negotiations.

Disadvantages of the English Situation

The English enjoyed few of these facilities. They were obliged in attempting to form alliances with the Indians to make long and difficult journeys by land—over rough and dangerous roads, consisting only of the paths made by the buffaloes through the woods or the trail of the Indian warriors; and when they reached the place where the council was to be held were comparatively much in the dark in respect to the true interpretation which they were to put upon the incidents that occurred, or the appearances that were presented, and to the course which it was proper to pursue to influence the decisions of the savage chieftains whose favor they were seeking.

Formation of the Ohio Company

The hold which the French had already obtained in the valley, by their traders and hunters, and by certain small military expeditions which they had sent into it from time to time to take possession of particular points, to build log forts and blockhouses, and to establish friendly relations with the Indians, was such as to render it unsafe for individual English settlers to attempt to go in alone and unprotected, and accordingly one of the first plans which was adopted by the governor and leading men of Virginia was to form a combination with a view of advancing into the country in considerable force. For this purpose a company was organized by a number of men of influence and of property in Virginia and Maryland in connection with a London capitalist, for organizing settlements on a considerable scale in the valley. The associates were incorporated under the name of the Ohio Company. They obtained a grant from the King of England of five hundred thousand acres of land to be selected by themselves in any part of the country west of the Alleghenies and on the banks of the Ohio. Among the other conditions of the grant to which the company agreed, they bound themselves to settle not less than one hundred families upon the land within seven years, and also to build a fort, and to garrison it with a sufficient force to defend their settlements from the Indians.

Employment of Washington by the Ohio Company

Lawrence Washington, George's brother, was one of the most prominent of the Virginia members of this company, and he took a very active part in the management of its affairs. Through him George Washington became greatly interested in it, and was employed by the company in various missions and negotiations, for which his knowledge and sound judgment in respect to land, and his familiarity with life in the woods, and with the habits and usages of the Indians, eminently qualified him.

He was also sent on several important missions at different times by the governor of the colony.

In the course of these expeditions he suffered many hardships and exposures, and met with many narrow escapes; but his prudence, his caution, and more than all, perhaps, the influence and effect of that calm and quiet energy, courage and self-possession, which so strongly marked his character, carried him safely through them all.

Appointment of George Washington to a Military Command

These various embassies and missions sent into the valley led to no result, except to show that the French were determined to insist upon their title to the country, and the Virginia government began to make vigorous preparations for war. Washington had taken so prominent a part in the preliminary operations, and had evinced such excellent qualities that, though he was not yet twenty years of age, he was appointed by the governor to take charge of the military organization of one of the districts into which the state was divided. His title was Adjutant-General. He was proposed for this appointment by his brother Lawrence, who continued to take the warmest interest in his welfare and advancement, and the governor conferred it without hesitation.

His Military Studies

Washington immediately engaged with great ardor in the performance of the duties of his office, which related to the work of organizing and equipping the militia of his district. At the same time he devoted himself very assiduously to the study of the art of war. There were among Lawrence Washington's acquaintances two former comrades of his who had returned with him from the West Indies and were living in Virginia. One was Adjutant Muse, an Englishman, and the other a Dutchman named Van Braum, who professed to be an accomplished swordsman, and who was at that time indeed gaining his livelihood by giving fencing lessons.

Washington immediately employed these men as his teachers. Adjutant Muse brought him books treating of military tactics and the maneuvers of bodies of men in the field, and gave him all necessary instruction and guidance in the perusal of them. Van Braum taught him fencing and other similar military arts. Washington devoted himself wholly to these pursuits, and the house at Mount Vernon assumed for the time being the appearance of a military station, where nothing was to be seen or heard but the going and coming of military messengers conveying orders, and the drilling of men in the exercises of arms.

Death of Lawrence Washington

These pursuits, however, were interrupted for a time by the sickness of Lawrence Washington, and by the departure of George with him on a voyage to the West Indies for the recovery of his health. Lawrence had been for some time in a decline, and his physicians now ordered him to a change of climate as the only means of saving his life. He wished to have his brother George accompany him, and George readily consented to do so. It was in 1752.

The brothers spent the winter in Barbados. Toward the spring Lawrence being somewhat better, but considering it still too early to return to Virginia, and feeling lonely and ill at ease under so long a separation from his wife, determined to go to Bermuda, and to send to Virginia to bring his wife to Bermuda to meet him there. George accordingly returned to Mount Vernon, and not long afterward Lawrence himself returned, with barely strength enough remaining to reach his home. He died a very short time after his arrival.

The bereavement involved in this event was for George like the death of a father. He had first come under the care of his brother while he himself was quite a child and his brother a full grown man, and ever since that time Lawrence had fulfilled toward him with great fidelity and sincere affection all the duties of a parent; and George looked up to him, as long as he lived, with a species of filial veneration.

Mount Vernon

After the death of his brother, George Washington became the head of the family at Mount Vernon, as the executor of Lawrence's will and the legal protector of his wife and infant daughter. His brother had made him also prospectively the heir to the property, which accordingly in due time descended to him. He thus at this time entered into possession of Mount Vernon and continued his possession—for a time as executor and guardian and afterward as proprietor—to the close of his life. There he died and there his remains have rested undisturbed to the present day.

Preparations for War

As it had become evident on all sides that the question of the title to the valley of the Ohio could only be settled by war, both parties immediately began to prepare for the contest. The Ohio Company commenced preparations for building a fort at the junction of the Monongahela and Allegheny where these two rivers form the Ohio, near the point where the town of Pittsburg now stands. The French advanced their posts into the disputed territory on several different lines, and built forts and blockhouses, and established military stations at all important points.

During the time while these preparations were in progress, both parties were busy in carrying on negotiations with the various tribes of Indians inhabiting the country, calling councils of the most influential chiefs, and sending them presents of such articles and commodities as they deemed most likely to please such savages—guns, powder, shot, knives, blankets, gaudy calicoes and cloths, cheap but showy trinkets, and, worst of all, rum. At these councils each party attempted to convince the Indians that they were their friends, and only wished to come into their country out of disinterested love for the red man and desire to benefit him, and that the other party were dangerous enemies to the Indians, men of reckless and desperate character, who wished to force their way into the region in order to dispossess the Indians of their lands, and who would not shrink from any treachery or cruelty to accomplish their ends.

Reluctance of the People of the Colony to Undertake the War

It was the royal governor of Virginia and not the legislature or the people of the province that chiefly urged on the work of expelling the French from the valley of the Ohio. The people of the province, with the exception of a comparatively small number of hunters and Indian traders, were contented with their own homes on the eastern side of the Alleghenies, and were not much disposed to incur the cost and submit to the great sacrifice of life which they foresaw would be inevitable, in a cause in which the extension and future glory of the

British empire was much more the object at stake than any direct or practical interests of theirs.

But the royal governor, acting as the royal governors of the province generally did, in the interest of the crown, and not in that of the people of the colonies, was eager in pressing on the preparations for war. The legislature were slow in responding to his urgency. They were reluctant to vote money or to raise men. They even made the governor indignant by seeming to doubt after all whether the English title to the valley was so absolutely clear as he regarded it. Finally, however, a certain sum was voted, and authority was given to raise men. The men were induced to enlist by promises of land when the possession of the country should be secured, and the awkward squads of rough farmers' boys and backwoodsmen which were thus recruited were organized, disciplined, and trained, as well as they could be, by Washington, with the assistance of Adjutant Muse, Van Braum and other such aids.

The Cooperation of the Other Atlantic Colonies Obtained

Governor Dinwiddie took active measures to secure the aid of the governors of the other colonies which lay contiguous, on their western border, to the valley of the Ohio—more particularly those of Maryland, Pennsylvania, and New York—and they all in the end took a more or less active part in the war. Some aid certainly, but with it a great deal of embarrassment and confusion of counsel, arose from the cooperation of so many distinct parties and powers in the conduct of the campaigns.

At one time during the course of the war a convention was held of no fewer than six governors of as many independent states to consult on the measures to be adopted, and to make the necessary arrangements for carrying them into effect. As the home government was also represented in this convention, we have here a congress of seven distinct and in some respects independent powers, all more or less suspicious and jealous of each other, and without any real head, to plan a military campaign—a work which of all human undertakings requires most absolutely the unity of purpose and design which can only be secured through the action of a single judgment, and the prompt resolution of a single will.

Interference of Jurisdiction and Authority during the War

Indeed the greatest source of delay, difficulty, and embarrassment from which the English and colonial armies suffered during the war, was the interference of jurisdiction and authority on the part of the powers which were engaged in prosecuting it. The home government made a distinction which they insisted on maintaining between the officers who received their commissions from the crown, and those who were in the colonial service—as they did also between the regular English troops which were sent out from England, and the colonial soldiers, which last the regular army looked down upon with something like contempt. Then the troops furnished by the different colonies, were under their own officers, who were each tenacious of his own authority and jealous of the others. During the whole course of the war of the revolution, Washington seems to have met with more serious embarrassment and with greater obstacles to his success from difficulties arising from such sources as these than from all the military operations of the enemy.

Difficulties of Being at the Same Time Many and One

The original settlement of this country by a very large number of distinct and separate colonies, resulting as it did in the establishment of so many distinct, and, for many of the functions of government, independent states, operates very decidedly for the benefit of the whole population in times of peace and general security, since it enables each separate community to shape its institutions and conduct its industrial pursuits in its own way, according to the varying tastes and habits of the people, or the differences of climate, soil, and other physical conditions under which they live. But it has always been a great source of embarrassment and difficulty in times of insurrection or war, and indeed in all cases where the combined action of the whole has been necessary to secure some common good, or to defend the country in general against some common danger. This evil was felt quite seriously in this war with the French and Indians, and still more seriously in the war of Independence, twenty years later, as we shall presently see.

General Course and Result of the War

The war which was commenced in the valley of the Ohio, in the manner thus described, was continued for many years. The general course and the final result of it have been described fully in the history of the wars of the colonies, given in a previous number of this series. It is sufficient here to say, that in all their operations in the valley of the Ohio, the original scene of the conflict, the English were for a long time entirely unsuccessful. Except in certain subordinate and restricted operations which were committed to Washington's charge, the narrative for several years relates little else than a series of disasters.

The French built and garrisoned a strong fort at the junction of the Monongahela and Allegheny, which they named Fort Du Quesne, in honor of the governor of Canada, and for a long time they resisted all the efforts of the British and colonial forces to dispossess them.

At length, however, in 1758, three years after the commencement of the war, the fort was taken, and as it formed in a great measure the key to the valley, the fall of it was a fatal blow to the French power in the western country.

The English moreover finally determined to attack the French dominion in North America at the head and center of it, and to make all end of it forever. They fitted out a grand expedition in England—a naval and military force combined—to cross the Atlantic, ascend the St. Lawrence, and attack the cities of Quebec and Montreal, with a view of totally subverting the French power on the continent. The attempt was successful. Quebec and Montreal fell, and with their fall the French power was destroyed, and then the whole country passed unquestioned into the power of the conquerors.

The Part Performed by Washington

Washington himself was engaged during the war only in the campaign on the Ohio, and though the operations in that region were so long unsuccessful, the part which he performed in them was marked by so much prudence, wisdom, courage and energy, that though the commanders under whom he served incurred much discredit for their failures, he himself acquired a great military reputation, not only among his countrymen in Virginia but abroad. It was a rare instance of military fame acquired by connection with campaigns and operations which ended almost entirely in disaster and defeat.

Nature of His Services

Sometimes detached commands for the accomplishment of special objects were committed to Washington's charge. These he managed successfully. And oftener still his coolness, self-possession, and quiet energy were called into requisition to save remnants of defeated bodies of men, after battles lost through the self-conceit or recklessness of the English officers his superiors. It was on an occasion when he held an independent command of a small body of men, on a sort of scouting expedition at the very commencement of the war, that he fought his first battle and gained his first victory, which, although the whole operation was on a very small scale, yet occurred at a time and under circumstances which attracted great attention to it, throughout the country, and formed quite a brilliant commencement to the military fame which he subsequently acquired.

Occasion of the First Battle and Victory

Washington was marching at the head of a small force through the woods toward the station at the junction of the Monongahela and Allegheny, which was the great object of contention at the beginning of the war, and where hostilities had already commenced. After going on for some days among forests and mountains, he learned

The Valley of the Ohio

Washington's first combat.

that a French force was hovering near him, watching no doubt for a chance to surprise him.

One dark and rainy night, about nine o'clock, some friendly Indians came into his camp and informed him that they had discovered where this French detachment were. They had encamped, they said, in a low bottom land, near the river, in a place shut in by rocks and thickets, and if he wished to attack them they offered to go with him and assist him. There was, moreover, a body of Indians not far away who were ready, they alleged, to join him in such an attempt.

Advance to the Attack

Within an hour from the time of receiving this intelligence Washington had aroused his men, organized a guard to be left behind to defend the camp, and was ready to commence his march with the rest. They moved on silently through the woods, in utter darkness, groping their way as well as they could along the Indian trail, in mud and rain. The force consisted of forty men.

The little column reached at length the camp of the Indians who were expected to cooperate with them. The Indians were all ready to join them. Washington then first sent on scouts to reconnoiter the French encampment, and finding everything favorable he led his men forward to the attack. The assailants advanced in two separate parties, each creeping cautiously through the woods in single file, the Indians in one line and Washington's men in the other.

The enemy, who had considered the security of their hiding place perfect, especially in such a night of wind and rain, were totally unprepared for their coming. Their surprise was complete. They, however, rushed to their arms and attempted to form and defend themselves. The contest, in fact, continued for about a quarter of an hour, when their leader being killed, and quite a number of the men having also fallen, the rest fled, in hopes of finding the means of concealment or escape in the surrounding forest. They were, however, soon overtaken and made prisoners.

Washington treated his prisoners with great kindness, attending carefully to the wounded, and supplying the wants of the two surviving officers from his own private means. He sent them all to Virginia. Their arrival excited great attention, and brought Washington very conspicuously before the people of the colony. The number of prisoners, including the two officers, was twenty-one.

Return of Washington to Private Life

Washington took a very active and conspicuous part in the operations which in the end resulted in the capture of Fort Du Quesne, by which the war, so far as Virginia was concerned, was substantially closed. He then resigned his commission, and returned to Mount Vernon a private citizen—highly respected and honored, not only by the people of Virginia but throughout the whole land, on account of the very important services that he had rendered, and the exalted qualities which he had displayed.

CHAPTER III
LIFE AT MOUNT VERNON

The Young Widow

About the time of Washington's leaving the army and returning to civil life in his home at Mount Vernon, he was married. The circumstances under which his engagement to the lady was formed were somewhat romantic.

It was in 1758, near the close of the period of his military service, that he had occasion to make a journey to Williamsburg, the capital of the state, on some urgent business with the governor relating to the organization of the army. He traveled on horseback. In the course of this journey, through circumstances entirely accidental, he met with a very interesting young widow, then Mrs. Martha Custis, who, though at that time little aware of what was before her, was destined to become in the end a very renowned historical personage under the name of Martha Washington.

Crossing the Ferry

Colonel Washington, for that was then his title, made this journey, as has already been said, on horseback. In the course of it, and on his approach toward Williamsburg, he came to the river Pamunky, a branch of the York River. This river he was to cross, from the county of King William to that of New Kent, by a ferry, and then to go down on the southern side of the river to Williamsburg. He wore his usual military dress, which of course denoted his rank, and being also attended by a military servant was marked at once as a person of distinction. It happened that there was also on board of the ferry boat, making the transit of the river at the same time, a gentleman of the vicinity, a planter, who returning home from some short excursion reached the ferry at the same time with Washington. He was attracted by Colonel Washington's appearance, and entered into conversation with him; and at length as they drew near the shore, he earnestly invited Washington to stop and dine with him at his house which was not far off. Washington at first declined the invitation, saying that his business was urgent and that it was important that he should lose no time.

Mr. Chamberlayne, however—for that was the stranger's name—earnestly pressed him to accept the invitation, saying that it would detain him very little to stop an hour or two for dinner, and for the rest and refreshment of his horse, and that he might if he chose resume his journey immediately afterward. With this understanding Washington consented to the proposal, and on landing from the boat the whole party went together to Mr. Chamberlayne's house.

Mrs. Custis

They found some company here, and among the guests was Mrs. Custis. Although she had two children and had been a widow about three years, she was still young and beautiful. She had dark hazel eyes and hair, her countenance was agreeable, her form was particularly graceful, and her manners and address were marked with that frank and winning cordiality which is often characteristic of the ladies of the southern states, and which places the stranger or the new acquaintance entirely at his ease in their company, and invests the lady herself with an indescribable charm.

The Acquaintance Agreeable

After dinner, Bishop, Washington's servant, according to the orders which he had received from his master on their arrival, brought the horses to the door, and there they remained a long time, while Washington continued in conversation with the young widow, and with the other guests. The time passed very pleasantly, and at length Washington was urgently pressed to send the horses away and spend the night at the house. This he finally consented to do. The horses were put up. Washington remained during the afternoon and evening with the family, and resumed his journey the next morning, after taking leave of his friends, and promising to visit Mrs. Custis at her residence.

The White House

The residence of Mrs. Custis was known as the White House—the name which in later times became the popular designation of the presidential mansion in Washington, on account of the color of the material—white marble—of which it is constructed. The White House of Mrs. Custis was situated in the immediate neighborhood of Mr. Chamberlayne's, and was the family mansion pertaining to a large and rich plantation left to Mrs. Custis by her husband.

In the course of a few months following Washington's first interview with Mrs. Custis at Mr. Chamberlayne's, he visited her several times at her residence, in passing to and fro, on journeys made necessary by the public business in which he was engaged, and it was soon understood throughout the wide circle of acquaintances and friends with which the parties were connected that they were engaged to be married.

Washington Elected a Member of the Legislature

Some months before this time, when Washington found that the period was drawing near for his retirement from the army and return to the pursuits and occupations of civil life, he had offered himself as a candidate for election to the legislature for the County of Frederic, in the valley of the Shenandoah. Winchester was the chief town of this county, and here Washington had had his headquarters for considerable periods at different times, so that in addition to the general military fame which he had acquired, he was personally known to most of the people of this district.

The elections in those days were conducted, it seems, in the English style; that is, it was customary for the candidates to meet large assemblies of the voters, convened in the streets and in other public places, to harangue them on questions of public policy, and to expound and vindicate the principles on which the speaker pledged himself to act if elected; and then, after the election, the successful candidate was placed in a chair and borne on the shoulders of his party friends, in a procession about the town, with acclamations of triumph.

Washington was away on a campaign at the time when the election came on. His superior officer gave him leave of absence in order that he might attend at the polls, according to the custom. He, however, declined to avail himself of this permission, and sent another gentleman as his representative. This proxy made the speeches, and gave the entertainments, and distributed the largesses usual on such occasions; and finally, after the election was carried in Washington's favor, he was borne about upon the chair by the triumphant party, and received the customary plaudits and acclamations in his principal's name.

Washington's Aversion to Public Speaking and to Occasions of Parade and Display

It is probable that Washington was very willing to escape being personally present at this scene, as he had no fondness for public exhibitions or parades of any kind, and he had no special facility in making speeches to popular assemblies, especially on occasions of ceremony and form, when no practical question was at issue.

So little was he, in fact, at this period of his life, accustomed to such performances, that when subsequently he went to take his seat in the legislature, he was placed in quite an embarrassing situation. The legislative body had determined to mark his entrance among them with some token of their respect for the distinguished military services which he had rendered to the colony; and when he appeared to take his seat, and the oath was about to be administered, the speaker, according to previous arrangement, received him with an address of compliment and welcome, to which it was of course proper that he should make some reply. He accordingly attempted to speak, but he soon became so embarrassed that he was utterly unable to proceed, and the speaker was obliged to interpose and invite him to take his seat, saying to him that "his modesty was equal to his valor, which was more than words could express."

The Marriage

The marriage of Washington took place early in January, 1759, at the White House, and was celebrated with all the festivities and rejoicings usually attendant on such an occasion in those days upon the great plantations in Virginia. Mrs. Custis's plantation was very large and very valuable; and in addition to this landed property her husband had left her and the children nearly two hundred and fifty thousand dollars in cash investments. Of this property one-third fell to Mrs. Custis and two-thirds to the children, but on the marriage of Washington the whole came into his possession as the husband of the lady, or into his custody as guardian of the children.

One of the children was a boy six years of age, the other a girl of four. These children grew up under the charge of their new father. The daughter afterward died at the age of nineteen, and the son in early manhood, leaving descendants however, now well-known in Virginia.

Establishment at Mount Vernon

The White House was not very far from Williamsburg, then the seat of government of Virginia, and during the time that the legislature continued in session, which was about three months, Washington made his home at the residence of his bride. At the end of that time he took her with him to Mount Vernon, and there they lived together in peace and happiness for many years.

Plantation Life

Life on a plantation is always characterized by striking peculiarities, and these peculiarities were more strongly marked in those days than they are now. There were then no manufactories of any kind in America. The policy of the British government had always been to prevent by every possible means the fabrication of anything whatever in this country, with a view of compelling the people to depend upon the merchandise of England for their supplies of every kind, except agricultural products raised by the cultivation of the ground.

The result was that the Virginia planters could neither produce themselves nor easily procure anywhere in this country, anything for their families and their laborers but food. They depended for everything else almost altogether on the tobacco which they could raise and send to the English market.

SYSTEM OF COMMERCIAL EXCHANGE

The small farmers usually sold their tobacco to the merchants in the seaport towns, and procured supplies for their families from the very moderate stocks of foreign goods which these merchants had imported and kept on hand. The planters who owned large estates and many slaves, operated on a greater scale. They sent their crops of tobacco directly to England—sometimes in their own vessels —and imported in return directly to themselves the foreign articles which they required.

PRACTICAL INCONVENIENCES OF THE SYSTEM

Of course with such a mode of doing business, the members of a family to be supplied could have very little opportunity of selection in respect to the articles which they required, and very little control over the returns they were to receive, either in regard to quality or price; and in case of any dissatisfaction it must have been an extremely inconvenient and embarrassing circumstance that it required the sending of a complaint a distance of three or four thousand miles, and the lapse in time, of several months, to obtain redress.

Washington was remarkable during every period of his life for the method and system which he observed in the conduct of all his business affairs, and the care with which all his papers were arranged and preserved. There remain at the present day at Mount Vernon, files of his correspondence, and among them are various letters to and from his London agent, which give us a very distinct idea of the manner in which the business was conducted, and also preserve some specimens of the complaints for which the remissness or unfaithfulness of the London agents not unfrequently gave occasion. The following letters somewhat abridged are examples:

Specimens of the Correspondence

"Williamsburg, 1 *May*, 1759.
"To Robert Cary, Merchant, London.

"Sir,—The enclosed is the clergyman's certificate of my marriage with Mrs. Martha Custis, properly authenticated. You will therefore for the future please address all your letters which relate to the affairs of the late Daniel Parke Custis to me, as by marriage I am entitled to a third part of that estate, and am invested likewise with the care of the other two-thirds by a decree of our General Court, which I obtained in order to strengthen the power I before had in consequence of my wife's administration.

"At present this serves only to advise you of the above change, and at the same time to acquaint you that I shall continue to make you the same consignments of tobacco as usual, and will endeavor to increase them in proportion as I find myself and the estate benefited thereby.

"On the other side is an invoice of some goods which I beg you to send me by the first ship bound either for the Potomac or to the Rappahannock, as I am in immediate want of them. Let them be insured, and in case of accident, re-shipped without delay. Direct for me at Mount Vernon, Potomac River, Virginia. The former is the name of my seat, and the other of the river on which it is situated."

About a year after this he had occasion to write substantially as follows:

"By this conveyance you will receive invoices of such goods as are wanting, which please to send as there directed by Captain J., in the spring, and let me beseech you to give the necessary directions for purchasing them *upon the best terms*. It is needless for me to particularize the sorts, qualities or taste I would choose to have them in, unless my directions are observed; and you may believe me when I tell you that instead of getting things good and fashionable in their several kinds, we often have articles sent us that could only have been used by our forefathers in days of yore.

"It is a custom, I have some reason to believe, with many of the shopkeepers and tradesmen of London, when they know goods are bespoken for exportation to palm sometimes very old, and sometimes very slight and indifferent ones upon us—taking care at the same time to advance ten, fifteen, or perhaps twenty percent upon them in price."

The Estate at Mount Vernon

Although Washington continued to have charge of the plantation at the White House which now belonged jointly to him and the two children, his established home was from this time the estate at Mount Vernon, and a more delightful residence for a gentleman possessed of wealth and fond of rural occupations and amusements it would be difficult to imagine.

The estate was very large, extending for miles along the bank of the river, and comprising every variety of soil and scenery. There were beautiful lawns bordered and adorned with copses of trees and shrubbery near the mansion, and extensive fields of arable land, for the cultivation of corn and tobacco, and wide tracts of forest land, well stocked with deer, foxes, partridges, pigeons, and other game. There were hamlets of cottages, and cabins occupied by the overseers and laborers scattered here and there, with winding roads leading through most picturesque and varied scenery from one to another, and granaries for the storage of corn, and presses and warehouses for packing and preserving the crop of tobacco.

The mansion was situated upon a gentle swell of land near the river, sufficiently elevated to command a wide and charming view. It was spacious and convenient, and was amply provided with all the appointments and appurtenances necessary for the uses of a numerous family and for the parties of visitors which were often to be entertained there.

Nothing seems to be wanting to make such a plantation as this in such a climate, and so extremely profitable in its productions, a paradise upon earth, but the system of calling the laborers together on Saturday night, and paying them the fair and honest wages that they have earned—and the peace and mutual satisfaction and content which such a system brings with it.

Horses and Carriages

Washington's mind was of a cast which inclined him to simplicity and plainness in his habits and style of living, but such were the usages of those days among persons of wealth and distinction in Virginia—derived probably in a great measure from the influence of English manners upon them, through the intercourse of the colonists with English gentlemen of rank, many of whom as officers of the government or of the army, or landed proprietors, were much in this country at this time, and exercised a great ascendancy over fashionable society in all the colonies, and in none more so than in Virginia—that Washington in falling in with these usages to such an extent as was natural and proper for one in his position, lived in a style at Mount Vernon which would by no means be considered at the present day particularly simple and plain. He had an elegant carriage and four for the use of Mrs. Washington and her guests, with all the appointments and equipments of the most complete and fashionable character, according to the ideas and customs of London. The orders which he sent out for these things are still, many of them, extant in his letter books, and they show that he attached great importance, not only to the substantial quality of the articles ordered, for service and use, but to the freshness and fashionableness of them in respect to style.

In addition to his carriage horses he had in his stables an ample stock of saddle horses and hunters. In all his excursions and journeyings he was accustomed to go on horseback, having become greatly habituated to that mode of conveyance in the course of his military campaigns. Indeed any general officer after long service in active operations becomes so accustomed to his horse, that he often feels much more at his ease in the saddle than he does upon the cushions of any carriage.

Some idea of the figure which Washington made when mounted for the purpose perhaps of making a visit to some of his neighbors, or of accompanying his wife and children in a drive about the estate, may be formed from the items of the orders which he sent to England, about these days. In one of them he specifies "A man's riding saddle, large plated stirrups, and everything complete;—a double reined bridle and Pelham bit, plated;—a very neat and fashionable Newmarket saddle-cloth;—a large and best portmanteau;—a cloak bag, surcingle, checked saddle-cloth, and holsters;—a riding frock of a handsome drab colored broadcloth, with plain double gilt buttons;—a riding waist-coat of superfine scarlet cloth and gold lace, with buttons like those of the coat;—a blue surtout coat; a neat switch whip—silver cap; and a black velvet cap for servant."

Dogs and Hunting

Washington was fond of hunting, having acquired a taste for this amusement in his early intercourse with the Fairfax family at Belvoir, and at Greenway Court; and besides the horses adapted to this sport which he kept in his stables for the use of himself and his friends and visitors, he maintained a large number of dogs, in kennels built for the purpose; and in the proper season he used often to go out with them in pursuit of foxes, partridges, and other game. The estate comprised a large extent of woodland diversified with wild scenery of every kind, in the deep ravines and other shady recesses of which large numbers of wild animals found hiding places and food, and furnished for Washington and his guests abundance of game.

Fishing

The waters of the river, also, and of the various creeks and inlets that flowed into it from the grounds of the estate, abounded with fish of every kind. These waters were very extensive. Washington calculated that in all there was a length of *ten miles* of shore line washed by tidewater on his domain; so that not only could vessels of considerable burden come up directly to his wharf, to unload their cargoes of supplies for him, and receive in return the products of the estate, but there was also a wide range for navigation by boats between the different portions of the estate, and facilities were afforded for charming aquatic excursions. The planters living on the river used to provide themselves with handsomely ornamented boats for these purposes; with elegant appointments throughout, and crews of negroes, regularly uniformed, and trained as oarsmen, like a boatswain's crew of a man-of-war.

Busy Life

Although in comparison with military campaigns in the valley of the Ohio this life at Mount Vernon was quiet and retired, it was by no means an idle one. On the contrary, the daily routine of duty devolving upon Washington at this time, in the personal supervision of the Mount Vernon estate, in the general charge of the White House property, and in the public duties of various kinds which still devolved upon him, gave full occupation to all his powers, and made his life an extremely busy one.

The plantation itself of Mount Vernon was quite a little kingdom. It was divided into several distinct firms, each of which had its own separate set of laborers and superintendents, and its separate system of management and of accounts, according to the different articles of produce which the various divisions respectively afforded. Then there was timber to be cut in the woods and sawed into beams and boards for new buildings which were from time to time required; casks and barrels were to be made for the packing of tobacco and flour; smokehouses were to be built for the curing of bacon, which was one of the chief articles of food for the laborers; the tobacco was to be gathered, dried, and packed, the flour ground and barreled, and the casks and barrels, after being properly marked and branded, were to be shipped, the flour to the West Indies and the tobacco to London, and regular bills of lading to be made out and forwarded by mail. All this business was carried on under the close and constant supervision of Washington himself, with that perfect method and system, and that careful attention to details which so strongly marked his character. He kept all the accounts, inspected all the operations, watched for the appearance of every abuse, and kept every man up to his duty, in a fair and impartial, but in a very strict and energetic, manner.

Daily Routine at Mount Vernon

He rose early so as to obtain an hour or two before breakfast for writing and accounts. His breakfast was in winter at eight and in summer at seven. After breakfast he mounted his horse and rode around the estate to inspect the operations that were going on in the various departments. He went to the stables to see that the horses were properly cared for; to the kennels to bid good-morning to the dogs and to see them fed; to the fields where gangs of laborers were at work plowing the ground, or planting or hoeing the growing crops; to the forests where the slave carpenters were cutting or hewing timber; to the blacksmith's and cooper's and joiner's shops to see that everything was going right in them; to the different negro quarters to inspect the condition of the huts, and especially to visit any who might be sick, and to see to it personally that everything necessary for their comfort and for their recovery was supplied; and finally to reconnoiter the outer boundaries of the estate, in order to watch for and to warn off trespassers upon the forest, lands, or fishing grounds.

He returned to the house a little past noon for dinner, and then devoted the afternoon either to a continuation of the duties of the morning, or to work in his library upon his correspondence and accounts—or to accompanying his family in some visit to a neighboring plantation, or other excursion of pleasure.

At the close of the day the family met around the tea-table, and all retired early to bed.

Visits and Company

Notwithstanding the almost incessant demands which these numerous duties made upon the time and attention of Washington, he was still called upon by the usages of the country at that period to devote no small portion of many days to making and receiving visits, and to the duties of hospitality and of social intercourse. The visitors that he received were sometimes the families belonging to the neighboring plantations, or to more distant parts of Virginia, and sometimes English gentlemen—either persons officially connected with the government of the colony, or travelers who had come out to visit it for purposes of business or pleasure.

Belvoir

The place in the neighborhood where the Washington family were perhaps most intimate was Belvoir, the residence of Washington's early friend Sir William Fairfax. This estate, it will be recollected, was situated a few miles below Mount Vernon on the banks of the river, and the two families were at this time very intimate with each other. They interchanged many visits, and formed together hunting parties and boating parties and excursions of all kinds, in which very often distinguished visitors from the mother country took part, and were always prominent objects of interest and attraction to the native Virginians.

Visits to Annapolis

The nearest large town to Mount Vernon where fashionable life was exhibited on any considerable scale was Annapolis, then as now the capital of Maryland. Here in the winter season, when the legislature was in session, a very considerable circle of genteel society was accustomed to assemble, consisting of the members of the colonial government and their families, and wealthy country gentlemen of the neighborhood who often came with their wives and daughters to spend the winter in town. The brilliancy of this polite assemblage was sometimes much increased by the presence of English officers of the army or navy, casually present—visitors, perhaps, from a man-of-war anchored in the bay—or of English gentlemen of high position in the civil service of the colonies, or young men of rank connected with some of the many noble families who were in those days interested in making territorial acquisitions in America.

Washington often at this portion of his life went with his wife to Annapolis, during the season, to join in the fashionable festivities of the place. His wealth, and the high position which he occupied as a public man, made him an object of great interest and attraction in those polite circles, though it is said that he was too grave, dignified, and ceremonious in his manners ever to become a very great favorite with the ladies.

Public Duties

It must not be supposed, however, that during this period of his life Washington devoted his whole time to his private business and to the pleasures of social intercourse. He had still many public duties to perform which occupied no small portion of his time and attention. He was a member of the legislature, a judge in a county court, and he was vestryman in two parishes lying in the immediate vicinity of Mount Vernon. He seems not to have taken a very active part in the ordinary routine of business in the legislature, or in the everyday management of the affairs of the colony. But whenever any great question arose, or any important enterprise was to be undertaken, looking to substantial and permanent results, his action was energetic and decisive. Many examples of this kind might be adduced, but two or three must suffice.

Plan for Reclaiming the Dismal Swamp

One plan in which for a time he was greatly interested was the formation of a company for draining and bringing under cultivation the land of the Dismal Swamp, which is an immense tract of boggy ground on the confines of Virginia and North Carolina, not far from the sea. It is about ten miles wide and thirty miles long. Swamps of this kind are produced usually by subterranean springs rising in such abundance over a wide extent of territory that the natural outflow through the brooks and streams that issue from it is not sufficient to carry off the water. The surplus stagnates, forming all over the ground innumerable pools, bogs and quagmires, in which aquatic and semi-aquatic plants grow abundantly and reptiles without number breed. In process of ages the vegetable and animal remains that result accumulate often to a great depth, and form, when at last the whole is drained and brought under cultivation, a soil of great depth and of inexhaustible fertility.

Exploration of the Swamp

Washington was interested in a company formed for reclaiming this territory, and he went at the head of a small surveying party to explore it. Many portions of the ground are sufficiently hard to bear the weight of a horse, though in traversing it on horseback it is necessary to proceed with extreme caution, as there are many treacherous spots where an animal of such weight, once sinking in would become inextricably mired.

Washington, however, was thoroughly versed in everything relating to forest life, and he conducted the exploration in safety, camping at night upon such firm spots of ground as he could find. The examination which he thus made, and the steps taken by the company in consequence of it were the foundation of great improvements which have since been effected in this region—though the swamp has never yet been reclaimed.

EXPEDITION TO THE VALLEY OF THE OHIO

Another important undertaking in which Washington engaged at this period—one which, like his exploration of the Dismal Swamp, must have recalled very forcibly to his mind his old experiences of life in the wild woods, was an expedition which he made down the Ohio, with a view of selecting a tract of land to be allotted to his old comrades, the soldiers in the war with the French and Indians.

During the war Governor Dinwiddie, the governor of the state, had promised by proclamation, as an inducement for volunteers to enlist, that two hundred thousand acres of land should be set apart on the return of peace, to be divided among the officers and soldiers of the army. Washington was appointed one of the commissioners to settle these claims, and when at length, some time after the French had been expelled from the territory, the government succeeded in extinguishing the Indian title to a considerable portion of it, Washington set off on an expedition into the valley to select the tract to be set apart for this purpose.

ADVENTURES IN THE VALLEY

It was in 1770 that he set out on this expedition, a very few years before the breaking out of the revolutionary war. The party consisted at the commencement of Washington himself, Dr. Craik, a friend and neighbor who were to accompany him, and three negro servants—all mounted on horseback. They had besides a horse laden with baggage and provisions.

They pursued the usual route to the valley of the Ohio, directing their course first for the site of the old Fort Du Quesne, the name of which the English, since they had taken possession of the country, had changed to Fort Pitt, in honor of William Pitt, who was at that time the prime minister of England. They traveled twelve days through the woods and mountains before they reached Fort Pitt. Here they found that there was beginning to grow up quite a little town, which has since become the great iron-manufacturing and iron-working city of Pittsburg.

Voyage down the River

The party left their horses at Fort Pitt and took an Indian canoe for their voyage down the river. They also took some Indians with them to act as guides and interpreters, and to assist in navigating the canoe. They met with a variety of adventures on their voyage, and in visiting the establishment of the fur traders, and the different Indian villages that they passed on their way. They obtained their subsistence in a great measure from wild animals which they shot, such as deer that they saw from time to time browsing on the banks of the river, or coming down to the water to drink—and wild turkeys, and ducks and geese that abounded in the region.

Danger

The expedition was not entirely without the excitement of danger. Besides the ordinary hazards and exposures of traveling in wild and sometimes trackless woods, there was constant reason to apprehend hostility from the Indians, and still more, perhaps, from unprincipled white adventurers who were already beginning to penetrate into the valley, and to take possession of the lands, and who were of course very inimical to any party coming with governmental authority to survey and lay claim to the territory, and to put up metes and bounds. Still, though the travelers had frequent occasion for alarm, and were obliged to be very cautious, and to act with great circumspection in their treatment of the Indians, they met with no serious disaster.

In the end Washington succeeded perfectly in accomplishing the object of his mission. He selected the lands to be apportioned among the soldiers and marked the boundaries of the tracts chosen, by suitable designations. Afterward, on his return to Virginia, the apportionment was made in due form, and each officer and soldier received his proper share.

Duration of the Period of Quiet Life at Mount Vernon

It was in 1758 that Washington first took up his permanent abode at Mount Vernon. He was married early in 1759. The troubles with the mother country commenced about 1765, and the war of the revolution which called Washington away from his home to take command of the American armies was formally opened in 1775. Thus the quiet period of his life, spent chiefly with his family, in peace and happiness at home, though varied by occasional absences on important public business of a civil nature, extended through a period of about fifteen years.

Movements that Preceded the Revolution

Several of the last years of this period were, however, considerably agitated by the difficulties and contentions that had then begun to arise between the colonies and the mother country in respect to the great question which was destined finally to separate them forever—namely, whether the control and the regulation of the colonial taxation rested with the colonial legislatures or with the English Parliament.

The civil part of this contest—which consisted of the discussions, and also of the legislative measures of coercion adopted by the government, and the countermeasures of resistance tried by the colonial legislatures, and by voluntary combinations of the people—continued during a period of ten years before the result was reached of open war. Washington from the beginning took decided ground on the side of the colonists, acting, however, in all the measures which he recommended, with the calmness and deliberation so characteristic of him. The influence which he exerted in uniting the people of Virginia, especially the rich and influential families, in the determination to assert firmly the rights of the colonists, and to make arrangements for vigorously maintaining them, was very powerful.

Meeting of the First Continental Congress

At length when in 1775 the first congress of delegates from the several colonies was called to meet at Philadelphia, for the purpose of organizing united action, Washington was elected as one of the delegates from Virginia, and at the opening of the meeting he appeared as one of the most distinguished of the many very able and eminent men which that body contained. The high military reputation which he had acquired in the wars with the French and Indians, his wealth and exalted social position, his mature age, his tall and commanding person, his calm, thoughtful and cautious, but resolute and determined character, and his simple and unpretending, though grave and dignified bearing, combined to make him one of the most prominent men in the assembly.

Appointment of Commander-in-Chief

When at length hostilities were commenced by the battle of Lexington, and the whole country began to rise in arms, it devolved upon the Continental Congress to combine and organize the resistance which the united colonies were to make, and one of the first measures to be adopted was to appoint a commander-in-chief of the forces to be raised.

Washington was at once regarded by everyone as the most prominent candidate for this office. He had been from the beginning the leading man in Congress in respect to all military affairs. There were, however, other candidates proposed, and some objection was made to the appointment of Washington, on the ground that the chief force then existing consisted of New England men that had assembled in large numbers around Boston, forming an army there of twenty or thirty thousand men, and it seemed to be somewhat uncertain how they would like to have a southern man sent to command them.

After full consideration, however, all these objections were overruled, and Washington was appointed to the office by a unanimous vote.

Farewell to Mount Vernon

Washington very naturally concluded that his wife would hear at Mount Vernon of her husband's being called to a position, which though one of great honor, would necessarily expose him to great hardships and to much danger, and would for a long time separate him almost entirely from her and from the home where they had enjoyed together so many years of tranquility and happiness. In writing to her, to communicate the tidings, he assured her that he had done nothing to seek, but everything that he could properly do to avoid having this duty assigned him. But he had been led to it, he said, by circumstances under divine providence wholly beyond his control, and he could not refuse to accept the trust and undertake the service to which he was thus called, without manifest dereliction of duty.

He mourned the necessity of bidding farewell for a time to the scenes of quiet happiness which he had so long enjoyed at Mount Vernon with his wife and family, and expressed a confident hope that Mrs. Washington would acquiesce cheerfully in the unavoidable separation. He charged her not to disquiet herself with vain regrets and unnecessary anxieties and fears; but to make herself happy with such means of enjoyment as still surrounded her, and to await with fortitude and hope the return of their former happy days.

CHAPTER IV
THE REVOLUTION

Qualities Necessary in a Commander-in-Chief

One might easily imagine that the prime and essential qualities of a commander-in-chief for a great army would be the knowledge of military tactics and strategy necessary to enable him to maneuver his forces properly before the enemy, and valor in leading them into battle. But Washington soon found that the possession of such qualities as these, on which success in actual fighting depends, constituted but a small and comparatively insignificant part of what was required of him in executing the trust which Congress had imposed upon him. Nearly a year was spent, after he entered upon the duties of his office, in the most arduous, incessant and harassing labors and cares, requiring patience, steadiness, very extended knowledge of facts, great skill in dealing with men of all varieties of character, and mental resources of the highest order—almost before any occasion occurred for firing a single gun in actual combat. These were the times and these the services that tried his fitness for the position most severely.

Incipient Difficulties

When Washington was appointed commander-in-chief, the only part of the country where hostilities had already commenced, and where the Americans had assembled any armed force, was in the vicinity of Boston. There a confused and unorganized mass of twenty or thirty thousand men had hastily come together, and to that point Washington accordingly at once proceeded, to assume command. He made his headquarters at a large and convenient house in Cambridge, and here he remained for nearly a year—struggling incessantly with difficulties, obstacles, and embarrassments that would have overwhelmed almost any other man, and which repeatedly reduced Washington himself very nearly to despair.

Conflicts of Authority

One of the greatest of these sources of embarrassment and difficulty—one, too, which he encountered in all its force at the very outset of his undertaking, and which continued to be an occasion of trouble and perplexity during the whole period of the war—was the conflict of authority and the disputes about precedence among the different divisions of troops and the officers commanding them. Washington found in the camps about Boston bodies of troops from several different colonies, and officers placed in command by various sources of authority, such as colonial legislatures, committees of safety appointed by large towns, and volunteer associations. In some cases bodies of men who had hastily come together, on the call of some influential man among them possessed of some military knowledge, had elected their officers by ballot. In other cases men who had raised a troop took command of it as a matter of course without any particular authority other than that conferred by the acquiescence of their followers.

All these men were willing to acknowledge Washington as commander-in-chief, he holding his office from the Continental Congress at Philadelphia; but in assigning to them their several positions and their relative rank under him, endless jealousies arose which gave rise to innumerable disputes and a great deal of ill will. It required on the part of Washington an extraordinary degree of tact, judgment and discretion, and a great deal of very wise and skillful management, to adjust all these conflicting claims and prevent open outbreaks.

Mrs. Washington's Visit

He was assisted very much in soothing the jealousies among his officers, and in cultivating kind and friendly feelings among them, by the tact and courtesy of Mrs. Washington, who made a visit to him at his headquarters in Cambridge during the fall of 1775. He had led her to hope, when he was appointed to the command of the armies early in the summer, that he should be able to return to Mount Vernon in the fall; and when he found, as the autumn came on, that there was no probability that he would be released during the winter, he sent to invite her to come to Massachusetts and visit him in camp.

Mount Vernon in Danger

Another reason why Washington desired that his wife should come to him, was because such was the state of things in Virginia that it was no longer safe for her to remain at Mount Vernon. Lord Dunmore, the British governor of Virginia, was beginning to adopt very decided measures to crush out the spirit of rebellion in that colony, and was proceeding very vigorously against all the people there within his reach, that he supposed to favor the cause of the colonies. Mount Vernon being on the banks of the Potomac, was exposed to receive a visit at any time from a man-of-war, and there was thought to be danger that Lord Dunmore might send a vessel up the river to destroy the place, and also perhaps to capture the family with a view of holding them as hostages, or otherwise making use of his possession of them to restrain or control the action of the commander-in-chief.

Arrival of Mrs. Washington at Cambridge

Mrs. Washington made the journey from Virginia to Massachusetts in a style comporting, according to the ideas of those times, with the rank and position of her husband. It was considered much more essential then than now—and especially so in Virginia—to mark the distinction of rank and wealth with appropriate symbols, in respect to dress and equipage and ceremony. These ideas were derived in the first instance from England where they still prevail, and they acquired a great ascendancy in those days among the aristocratic families of Virginia. Washington himself when he came on from Philadelphia to take command of the army, traveled in considerable state—being accompanied by a military escort, and received with

American History Vol. VIII

Arrival of Mrs. Washington in camp.

parade and military honors at all the large cities through which he passed. His headquarters were established at a large and handsome house in Cambridge, and he maintained in his mode of life there those observances of ceremony and etiquette, and formalities of parade which were demanded by public sentiment in those days in the case of persons occupying an elevated position in society, and especially in those exercising an exalted command.

Mrs. Washington made her journey in a private carriage, drawn by four horses. The horses were driven by black postilions dressed in an elegant livery of scarlet and white. She was accompanied by her son, and his wife—for her son had grown to manhood and been married, though her daughter had died.

She was received on her arrival with military honors, and was welcomed by the soldiers of the army and by the people of the vicinity, with loud acclamations.

Influence of Mrs. Washington in Camp

The presence of Mrs. Washington at her husband's headquarters exerted a very important influence in soothing the jealousies of the various officers, and producing harmony and good feeling among them. This effect was the result of the courtesy and kindness which marked her demeanor toward them, and the tact which she displayed in apportioning her hospitality and her attentions among them with some proper regard to their relative rank and influence, and in such a manner that none were neglected. Before she came, Washington himself had little time to attend to such details, and the invitations which he gave his officers to dinner parties, or to other entertainments at his house, according to the usages of a military camp in those days, were not so nicely regulated as always to avoid giving rise to jealousies and wounded feelings on the part of certain sensitive persons who sometimes imagined themselves neglected.

The general himself could only regret that men of sense engaged in so great a cause could allow their minds to be disturbed by such petty considerations of etiquette and punctilio. But Mrs. Washington removed the temptation from their minds by so arranging and regulating the mode and measure of her husband's hospitalities as to produce general satisfaction and good feeling.

CALLS FOR HELP AND PROTECTION FROM THE COAST

Washington himself, moreover, had difficulties of a much graver character than these to contend with. One of the most serious of his perplexities was caused by the demands which soon began to come to him from various points along the sea-coast, for detachments from the army to protect towns exposed to incursions from the enemy, made either for the purpose of obtaining forage, or supplies, or to harass and distress the inhabitants. As soon as the British commanders found themselves surrounded in Boston, and hemmed in there by so large an insurrectionary force that it was not prudent for them to attack it at once in the open field, while yet it cut them off from all supplies from the country, they began to send out small expeditions along the coast, in vessels of war, with orders to procure supplies and in case of resistance to burn the towns. The places exposed to these attacks naturally desired to be protected, and urgent demands began to pour in upon the commander-in-chief that he should send detachments of troops to this place and that, to prevent the landing of the forces from the vessels.

These calls Washington was compelled to refuse. He had scarcely force enough to hold his ground against the army in Boston, and the places exposed were so numerous that to have attempted to guard them all would have required the dispersion of his whole force along the coast, leaving the interior of the country open to the advance of the British army. The refusal, however, produced a great deal of discontent and ill-feeling. "Why did we," said the people along the sea-board, "send our sons and brothers to keep guard around Boston, and leave our own towns and our own homes entirely unprotected and exposed?"

INSUBORDINATION AND UNMANAGEABLENESS OF THE MEN

In addition to these troubles the condition of the army itself was such as to fill the mind of the general with great and constantly increasing anxiety. At the first alarm that was sounded through the country, on the occasion of the battle of Lexington, great numbers of young and ardent men seized their arms and hastened to camp. But no one had any idea that this insurrectionary movement was to be the commencement of a long war. The separation of the colonies from the mother country was not at all intended, at this time, and the only aim of the rising, so far as any definite conception of the object in view was formed by the people at large, was to make such a demonstration of the fixed purpose of the people not to submit to taxation by Parliament, as to induce the government to abandon the policy.

They therefore, in seizing their arms and rushing to the vicinity of Boston, expected only to be absent from their homes a few days or weeks—and when they found that the case was assuming the form of a settled and permanent state of hostility, and that they were to be organized into a regular army, to serve for a long term, and to be subjected to strict discipline, they became almost wholly unmanageable.

There was among them an abundance of that ardor and enthusiasm that is aroused by any exciting emergency, suddenly occurring and soon to pass away; and they were, also, as their conduct at Lexington and Bunker Hill fully evinced, courageous and resolute in coming up promptly to any real work assigned them, and standing firmly to it, in the midst of the most appalling danger—but to be called upon as they now were to give up all that had been dear to them in life, to surrender their liberty, their independence, and everything like freedom of action, for no one knew how long, and bend their necks under the yoke of that rigid discipline and that dull routine of confinement, privation, humiliating submission to petty authority, and inglorious hardship and exposure which constitutes the ordinary life of the soldier entering upon a long campaign, was a demand upon their patriotism for which they were wholly unprepared.

It seemed for a time impossible to remedy the evils of this state of things. No gentle measures could ever reduce such a heterogeneous mass of independent, free thinking, and free speaking men to an organized and efficient army—and any harsh measures would drive them altogether away.

No Ammunition

Another source of difficulty and danger, which might by the merest accident have proved fatal to the cause, was the almost total destitution of the army, if army it might be called, of ammunition and of military stores. Of course the first duty which devolved upon the general in taking command was to arrange the system of organization, and to distribute the different bodies of troops at the various points along the line held by them, in order to guard, at every point, against a sudden attack from the enemy. In making these dispositions Washington had called for a return of the quantity of gunpowder on hand, and by some mistake the whole quantity which the province had procured at the outset was reported as the amount then on hand—when in fact almost the whole of it had been expended at Lexington and Bunker Hill. At length, however, in making a call for a quantity of cartridges to supply the troops at a particular point, Washington discovered to his great alarm, it might almost be said to his consternation, that there was not powder enough in his whole army, even for a considerable skirmish. If the British had been aware of the state of things they could have marched out of Boston and advanced upon any part of his lines, and after receiving the first fire would have found the whole colonial force entirely in their power.

Necessity of Remedying These Evils without Making Them Known

The worst feature of the situation in which Washington was placed, was that it was necessary to contrive some way of remedying these evils without making them known. Of course if the British commander in Boston should obtain any glimpse of the real state of things in the American camps, he would at once have made a general attack upon them, and Washington knew very well that there were plenty of persons all around him to give the information if once it should transpire. There were a great many people at this time—many of them wealthy, influential, and well-informed—that secretly or openly sympathized with the British government, and wished that the rebellion should be put down. The lines had not been then distinctly drawn, and no one knew certainly who were friends or who were enemies. It was, therefore, not safe to reveal such a secret as the total want of ammunition in the army to any one; far less to communicate it to any legislative body or executive committee in any one of the colonies. Washington did not dare even to make known the destitution and disorganization of his army to the Continental Congress, but was obliged to call upon them very urgently for means of remedying difficulties and averting dangers, the very existence of which he was obliged carefully to conceal from them.

Washington Almost in Despair

The difficulties and embarrassments with which the commander-in-chief thus found himself surrounded became so great in the course of the summer, and all the efforts which he made to provide remedies for them were so utterly baffled, that he was at last reduced almost to a state of despair. In some of his letters to a confidential friend he said that his anxiety caused him many sleepless hours at night, when all around him were in repose; and that if he had known the difficulties and trials which he should be called to encounter, he should have greatly preferred to have shouldered his musket and taken his place in the ranks; or, if he could have reconciled such a course with his sense of duty to his country, he should have been far happier to have abandoned everything, and have retired with his family into the wilderness and lived there, like the Indians, in a wigwam, than to have assumed the command.

Discontent and Dissatisfaction of the People

The worst of the trials which he had to endure was the discontent of the people, and the many complaints which they made of his inefficiency and inactivity, all of which he was obliged to endure in silence, since the causes which made any decisive action impossible could not be explained to them. It was an exceedingly severe trial for a man of so lofty a spirit as Washington, and one accustomed, as he had been for many years, to receive every possible mark of consideration and honor from his fellow men, to be obliged to rest quietly for many months under undeserved censure, and to be the object of general dissatisfaction and complaint from which he could only defend himself by revelations that would greatly jeopardize the cause intrusted to his care. It was that peculiar cast and quality of mind which enabled Washington in circumstances like these to bear this obloquy, and keep his own counsel, and patiently persevere in the laborious, discouraging, and unrequited exertion necessary to overcome the difficulties of his situation, which, far more than the military skill required for the maneuvering of armies, and the courage evinced in leading troops into battle, constituted the crowning glory of the great chieftain, and made him the successful instrument of establishing the independence of his country.

Final Triumph of the Army before Boston

Washington was obliged to bear up as well as he could under these difficulties and trials through all the summer and autumn of 1775, and the winter of 1775–6; but at length, in the following spring, the time of action and of triumph came. Active operations were commenced; the result was that the British were compelled to evacuate Boston, and the country was everywhere filled with triumph and joy. The character of Washington and the wisdom of his measures were for the time fully vindicated, and the general confidence of the community in his eminent fitness for the supreme command was restored.

The Contest for the Possession of New York

After the evacuation of Boston the scene of military operations was transferred to the vicinity of New York, and here Washington had substantially the same course of experience to pass through as at Boston. But a small portion comparatively of the forces that had been under his command at Boston could be transferred to the new sphere of operations, and still less could the organization of it be preserved. A new combination was made of new elements, and new difficulties were to be encountered, or rather the old difficulties presented themselves in new aspects and with new force. There was the same embarrassment from the jealousies and conflicting claims of the officers coming from the different colonies, and from the sectional prejudices and mutual animosities of the men; the same conflict of authority among the various governments represented; the same scarcity of supplies and munitions of war; and the same stern and invincible necessity of concealing deficiencies and wants, which, notwithstanding, could only be supplied by being made known.

Washington Is Overpowered by the Difficulties of His Situation

The consequence was that with the utmost exertion Washington could not make a stand against the pressure of the vastly superior force of the enemy. He was driven back from one after another of the defenses of New York, until the city and all the adjacent waters, with the forts and batteries which had been built to defend them, fell entirely into the enemy's hands. Even here the tide of ill fortune did not cease to flow. His army was driven across the Hudson into New Jersey, and thence from post to post across the whole state of New Jersey into Pennsylvania.

A Party Beginning to be Formed against Him

The consequence of this long series of disasters was the gradual formation of a party in the country disposed to question his qualifications for the high command that had been entrusted to him. He was too cautious, too slow to act, too fearful of risk. For such times and for such a work a man of greater resolution and energy was required, they said, and secret movements began to be made for removing him and putting a more capable man in his place.

The People not to be too Severely Censured for Their Doubts And Misgivings

With the strong light which in later times has been thrown upon Washington's situation, and upon the difficulties which he had to encounter and the resources which he could employ, it is now universally admitted that he did all that it was possible to do with the means at his command during the whole of this trying period, and we are at the present day strongly disposed to censure the fickleness of the public mind which was so inclined to abandon him because he could not accomplish impossibilities. But the people judged then from the light which they had, and that light was not sufficient to show whether this long series of disasters was the result of incompetence in the commander, or of causes beyond his control. They judged by the immediate and apparent result, which is, after all, the only criterion by which military men can ever be judged by the general public that is contemporary with them.

The Character of Washington Retrieved

At length the time came for a change in the aspect of affairs. The opportunity arrived, and Washington availed himself of it by crossing the Delaware in the night, in boats pushed through the floating ice, and gaining an important victory under circumstances which showed to all mankind that he was ready for the most daring and energetic action when the occasion arrived that called for it. This first victory was followed by a series of others, in the course of which the British troops were driven back in their turn across the whole state of New Jersey, and finally expelled from the state entirely. Washington's fame was a second time vindicated, and all opposition to him was again completely silenced.

Character and Motives of Washington's Enemies

It was silenced but not destroyed. For, as is always the case with persons holding high command and having the disposal of many offices and honors, he had rivals who became enemies only because they *were* rivals—that is, they wished for his place, in order that they might themselves exercise his power and dispense his patronage; and in their efforts to remove him it was of course necessary for them to assume an attitude of hostility themselves, and do all in their power to create a hostile public sentiment against him.

The party who took this antagonistic position against Washington contained many men of high position, and of much influence, both in political circles and in the army; but so long as Washington's measures were successful they were powerless. In triumphing over the public enemy he triumphed over them also, for they could do nothing except so far as they could carry public sentiment with them. They could only at such times withdraw from notice and remain silent, to bide their time.

The general public changed their opinion of the commander-in-chief as his fortunes changed, but these men did not change; for the case with them was not that they wished to remove him because they thought him incompetent—but they wished him to prove incompetent in order that he might be removed. When after a long and discouraging struggle he came out triumphant in the end, the *people* were pleased to find themselves mistaken, for it revived their hopes of the salvation of their country. The factious leaders, on the other hand, were disappointed and chagrined at his triumphs, for it destroyed, for the time at least, their hopes of possessing themselves of his place and power.

THE THIRD DARK PERIOD OF THE REVOLUTION

The third dark period of the revolution through which Washington was called to pass—the darkest, indeed, of all—was the winter of 1777–1778. After the British had been driven out of the state of New Jersey, and the great army of Burgoyne, coming down from Canada, had been surrounded and captured by the forces under General Gates, as fully narrated in the preceding volume of this series, the seat of the war was transferred to Philadelphia and its environs. Washington made every possible exertion to defend that city; but after a long and cruel struggle his troops were forced back from one position after another, until Philadelphia itself and all the neighboring waters fell into the hands of the enemy; and Washington and his men were reduced to a condition of discouragement, destitution and suffering that was all but desperate. The difficulties and dangers which were surrounding and overwhelming the army seemed utterly irremediable. Congress had exhausted all its resources, and more than exhausted its credit. The men were half destitute of arms, of clothing, of food and of fuel, and there seemed no possible means of supplying any of these wants. Various governors were clamoring for troops to be sent to this point and to that to protect places exposed. The camp was filled with angry quarrels among the officers and mutinies among the men.

Indeed, if men ever could have an excuse for mutiny and desertion, the troops in Washington's camp might well claim to be lightly judged. They were encamped in wretched huts at Valley Forge, in mid-winter, with very little fuel, bad and wholly insufficient food, great numbers of them barefooted, and so scantily supplied with clothes that they were obliged to take turns in wearing the outside garments necessary to keep them from perishing when they went into the woods to obtain fuel for their fires.

In a word the past campaign had been disastrous and there seemed to be no possible glimmer of hope that anything better was to come. A general feeling of gloom and despondency prevailed throughout the land.

The Opposition Revived

Of course this state of things gave to the enemies of Washington a new opportunity. The combination against him was revived, and became more extended, determined, and persistent than ever.

No doubt a great many of those who joined in the movement honestly believed that Washington, though an excellent man in all moral points of view, and endued with many highly meritorious qualities of heart and mind, did not possess the commanding abilities, nor the energy, decision, and vigor required for so eventful a crisis, and they joined their influence with that which began to press for his removal, from honest and worthy motives. And even those who combined against him with a view of displacing him in order to bring themselves into power, were probably not actuated by any real feeling of ill-will or hatred against him, or by any other specially malignant motives. We may call it selfishness if we choose, and a desire of personal aggrandizement, for no lofty or noble ends—but it was only human nature after all in its normal and ordinary action, and not any special and particularly monstrous wickedness which led them to act as they did.

Such an Opposition Unavoidable

In every case where a man is raised to a lofty position, and is engaged in a great work which puts him in possession of extended power, he is always surrounded by a class of men who consider themselves next to him in the line of promotion, and who will be advanced in case he fails and gives way; and who, of course, have a direct interest in watching him narrowly; and in taking advantage of any misstep which he may make, or of any long continued want of success he may meet with. They form thus, as it were, a natural and permanent opposition around him. He cannot complain of this. It is in the nature of things that it should be so. Indeed, it is probably *best*, all things considered, that it should be so.

Measures Resorted to by the Party Opposed to Washington

Some of the opponents of Washington at this time are accused of resorting to covert, underhand, and ignoble means to effect his downfall. They wrote secret letters to undermine public confidence in him, and resorted to many maneuvers, both in Congress and in the army, to organize, extend and strengthen the party against him. These, the friends of Washington at the time, and many historians since, have designated as intrigues. But the line of demarcation which both in politics and war separates honest operations, conducted with a proper degree of prudence and privacy, from unworthy intrigues, is not very clearly drawn. It is probable on the whole, that though the fiery trial of enmity and opposition through which Washington had to pass in the darkest periods of his history, was very painful and severe, it was not any more so than is inevitable, in such a world as this, for a person engaged in so great a work, and one attended by obstacles, difficulties, and discouragements so great and so long continued as to cause the scale to hang trembling in uncertainty in respect to the result, for so many years.

General Gates

The person whom the opponents of Washington were inclined to bring forward as their leader, or rather as the commander whom they wished to put in his place, was General Gates. General Gates was really a very able officer, and an honest and excellent man, and he held at this time a particularly conspicuous position before the country on account of his recent success in defeating the grand expedition of Burgoyne, and capturing the whole of his army. How far he was himself directly concerned in the efforts made for supplanting Washington, has been a matter of dispute. There would, however, be nothing derogatory to his character in

the idea that supposing the people of the country to be in favor of a more active, energetic, and decisive mode of conducting the war than Washington was pursuing, and to be disposed to bring him forward in the place of Washington to carry their wishes into effect, he was ready not only to acquiesce in their wishes, but to do what he could do honorably to facilitate the change.

He, however, made a solemn declaration at a subsequent period, that he had never been engaged in any plot or plan for the removal of General Washington, and that he did not believe that any such plot existed.

General Conway

The person, undoubtedly, who was most active in these maneuvers to supersede Washington, was General Conway. He was an Irishman by birth, but had served in the American army from an early period, and had acquired a high rank in it, and considerable influence. He worked very much in the dark—mainly by private conversation, and by confidential correspondence with leading men both in the army and in Congress; but he was exceedingly active, so much so that at a later period, when his secret agency in the affair was brought to light, the conspiracy received the name of Conway's Cabal. Many of the letters which he wrote were anonymous, and there were some forged letters purporting to be written by Washington himself, and which were calculated greatly to injure his character, and which Conway is supposed by many persons to have written.

For a time he seemed to make a good deal of progress in the work which he had undertaken, and parties were formed for and against Washington, which resulted in producing great excitement, and for a time threatened very serious consequences. In the end, however, the friends of Washington carried the day. He was retained in the command of the army. Some of the underhand and intriguing operations of Conway and his friends were discovered and exposed. The party was brought into discredit, and this dark and very threatening cloud passed away.

End of General Conway

Many private and personal quarrels arose out of this affair after the public excitement had subsided. Conway himself became involved in one of these collisions, which led to a duel in which he was very seriously wounded, and for a week or two it was supposed that the wound was mortal. Believing himself to be on his deathbed, he wrote a letter of apology to Washington, expressing his sorrow for what he had done. The letter was as follows:

Conway's Letter

"Sir:—I find myself just able to hold my pen for a few minutes, and I take this opportunity of expressing my sincere grief for having done, written, or said anything disagreeable to your excellency. My career will soon be over; therefore, justice and truth prompt me to declare my last sentiments. You are in my eyes the great and good man. May you long enjoy the love, veneration and esteem of these states whose liberties you have asserted by your virtues.

"I am, with the greatest respect,
"Thomas Conway."

This letter was written after the third of the dark periods in the history of the war had passed away, and Washington's policy and character was once more in the ascendant. The French government, which had secretly favored the rebellion from the beginning, were willing to take an open part in aiding it after the capture of the army of Burgoyne, and the alliance began now to produce its effect. A French fleet arrived in the American waters, and Lafayette and other French officers rendered an efficient cooperation with the forces on land. From this time the cause of the Americans went on more and more successfully, until at length the capture of another army, that of Cornwallis, at Yorktown, completed the discouragement of the English government and people, and disposed them to submit to negotiations of peace.

CHAPTER V
NEGOTIATIONS FOR PEACE

Chronology

It is desirable that the reader, in studying the history of the revolutionary war, should keep in mind the dates of some of the principal events which marked the progress and termination of it. The war commenced by the battles of Lexington and Bunker Hill, in the spring and early summer of 1775. The first great success of the American arms—the expulsion of the British troops from Boston—was achieved about a year later, in the spring and early summer of 1776, and on July the Fourth of that year independence was declared.

The second and third great advantages gained, namely, the expulsion of the British from New Jersey, and the capture of Burgoyne's army, took place in 1777—the former in the winter and the latter in the autumn following, of the same year.

The treaty of alliance between the United States and France, through which the Americans received very important foreign aid, in men, in ships and in money, during the remainder of the war, went into operation in 1778.

The contest was continued after this principally in the southern states, through the years 1779, 1780, and 1781, with varying success, but chiefly to the advantage of the British, their forces advancing to the northward through South Carolina, North Carolina and Virginia, until at last their principal army, under Lord Cornwallis, was surrounded at Yorktown, in the fall of 1781.

This event virtually ended the active operations of the war. A period of negotiation ensued, which terminated, after many difficulties and much delay, in a treaty of peace, which was concluded in 1783, and by which the independence of the United States was acknowledged.

The nature of these negotiations, and the difficulties which attended them, will form the subject of this chapter.

COMPLICATED NATURE OF THE NEGOTIATIONS

The work of opening and conducting the negotiations was by no means so simple an operation as it might seem. In the first place there could be no direct communication between the parties. It is wholly beneath the dignity of any regularly constituted government to treat with rebels, or hold any direct official intercourse of any kind with them; and as long as the independence of America was not acknowledged by Great Britain, the Continental Congress, and all the forces under their control, it could be considered by the king and his government only as a band of rebels. Thus, even supposing that both sides were willing to make peace, there was this difficulty in the way, that the independence could not be acknowledged without some previous negotiation about terms and conditions—and this negotiation could not be commenced until the independence was acknowledged.

IMPLICATION OF OTHER GOVERNMENTS IN THE QUARREL

Besides this, the question could not be settled by the United States and England alone. There was not only the French government, which had been an open ally of the Americans during the latter portion of the war, and which was of course entitled to have its own interests recognized and provided for in settling the terms of peace, but there were other nations that had in one way and another been so far drawn into the quarrel that their interests were more or less involved in the settlement of it. The principal of these nations were Spain and Holland.

THE CASE OF HOLLAND

The circumstances under which Holland was drawn into the war were quite remarkable. Holland, like most of the other countries of Europe, was engaged in systems of policy which conflicted with those of England in various parts of the world, and her government had long secretly wished for the success of the American revolution, since it would tend to impair the power and prestige of Great Britain, but had not ventured openly to aid the insurgents. At length, however, in 1779, some secret correspondence took place between a member of the government of Holland, named Van Berkel and the American Congress, in consequence of which a commissioner was appointed to proceed to Holland with a view of endeavoring to negotiate a loan there for the purpose of raising funds, and also of obtaining from the Dutch government a recognition of American independence.

Henry Laurens

The commissioner appointed was Henry Laurens, a South Carolinian of wealth and distinction, who had taken a prominent part in the councils of the leaders of the revolution in America, and who had been for two years a member of the Continental Congress.

Capture of Laurens

Mr. Laurens sailed from this country in 1779 but the vessel in which he took passage was intercepted off Newfoundland, by a British frigate, and captured. When Laurens saw that the frigate was close upon them, and that it was impossible to escape, he went to his cabin and brought up a package containing all his papers and threw it overboard.

This movement was however observed on board the frigate, a boat was let down, and the papers recovered.

Laurens himself was immediately seized, and closely confined on board the ship. He was conveyed to London and imprisoned in the Tower, where he was quite harshly treated, being considered as a convicted traitor and rebel. He was not allowed the use of pen and ink, and was not permitted to hold intercourse with any friends in England who might be disposed to visit him.

He Remains Faithful and Firm

The harshness, however, with which he was treated is not to be attributed to a spirit of resentment, far less to wanton cruelty on the part of the British government, but rather to a motive of policy. Their design was to intimidate and discourage their prisoner, in the hope of inducing him in the end to abandon the American cause and aid the ministry, by his influence in America, in bringing the people to submission. He was twice approached with offers of liberty and large rewards if he would give up the contest. But he rejected these offers at once, and in the most decided manner.

The Capture of the Papers Leads to War between England and Holland

The package of papers which had been recovered from the sea proved, on examination in London, to contain the correspondence between Van Berkel and the American government, which showed very conclusively that the Dutch government was secretly aiding the rebellion. The English ministers were made very indignant by this discovery. They immediately demanded that the Dutch government should disavow the action of Van Berkel and dismiss him from office. This the government refused to do, and the English government then declared war against Holland.

Various Complications

The material interests of France and Spain were involved in the settlement of the question between England and America on account of Louisiana and Florida, between which and the territory which had belonged to Great Britain boundaries were to be fixed. In addition to these complications there were several perplexing questions in respect to the boundary line between the United States and Canada; for Canada, not having joined in the revolt, could not be included in the claim for independence.

There was, moreover, the great question of the fisheries on the banks of Newfoundland, which had long been a great source of wealth to the English people—employing as they did great numbers of vessels and men, and affording vast profits to all concerned in them.

Party Conflicts in Congress in Respect to the Appointment of Commissioners

The sending of commissioners to the different courts of Europe was a measure resorted to many years before the conclusion of the war, and the appointment of the commissioners led to serious and protracted conflicts in Congress. Besides the personal rivalries and contentions resulting from the ambition of individuals, the interests of the different sections of the country were not the same. The southern states felt naturally the greatest concern in respect to the understanding to be secured with France and Spain, on account of the boundary between them and the provinces of Louisiana and Florida, and the navigation of the Mississippi involved in that question, for the mouth of that river was in French territory.

The northern states, on the other hand, were more interested in the Canadian boundary, and the question of the fisheries of Newfoundland, in which the people of New England only were engaged. These questions and difficulties led to many very earnest contests among the political leaders, both in Congress and throughout the country at large, and could only be settled at last by a sort of tacit understanding that the appointments should be fairly proportioned among the different sections that were differently interested in the results.

The Commissioners

The principal persons who were engaged in the final negotiation of the treaty were Laurens, Adams, Franklin, and Jay. Laurens, after being confined in the Tower of London for more than a year, was liberated at last by the English government when they found that negotiations for peace must be commenced, and he had been sent to Paris to assist in the conduct of them. Franklin had been for some time in Paris, and Adams in Holland, while Jay had been engaged in negotiations in Spain. In due time, however, when the British government had finally found themselves compelled to open negotiations, these commissioners all assembled at Paris, and there the convention was finally concluded.

Of these commissioners Laurens might be supposed to reflect the views and opinions of the southern states, Adams those of New England, and Jay and Franklin those of New York and Philadelphia.

Benjamin Franklin

Of all these men Benjamin Franklin was the most distinguished among the upper classes of society on the continent of Europe, on account of his reputation as a philosopher. He had created a great sensation by some of his scientific discoveries, especially by his grand experiment of the electrical kite, by which he demonstrated the identity of origin in the electrical phenomena of the lecture-room and the thunder and lightning of the skies.

This identity had been suspected, but had not been proved until at length Franklin, in 1752, from a little tool-house in his garden near Philadelphia, sent up a kite into a thundercloud, and by means of a metallic thread in the string drew down the electricity from it, and produced the same effects with it, as the philosophers had been accustomed to produce with the electricity developed by their machines.

The fame of this experiment, joined to certain striking personal characteristics which marked the conduct and social intercourse of Franklin, made him very conspicuous at the time among the commissioners, though in respect to actual negotiation of the treaty history assigns the most prominent part to Jay.

Complications and Difficulties on the British Side

The complications and difficulties attendant on the negotiation of the treaty were not altogether confined to the Americans. There was a long struggle, accompanied by violent dissensions and disputes, in the British Parliament, before a majority was gained in favor of abandoning the war. Then when Parliament had been brought over, the king was extremely reluctant to acknowledge himself conquered by a rebellion. And when at length he finally yielded, a great many technical embarrassments and questions of etiquette and ceremony

Negotiations for Peace

Franklin and the electrical kite.

intervened, arising from the difficulty of opening negotiations for acknowledging the independence of a power, without virtually recognizing its independence by the very act of opening the negotiations.

The Question in Parliament

The only mode by which a change on the part of the British government in any great system of policy can usually be effected is by the party in Parliament, opposed to that policy, gradually increasing until it becomes a majority. When this occurs the ministry must resign, and a new ministry, composed of men in favor of the new measures, must be appointed in their places, for it is impossible for the government to be carried on without the concurrence of the House of Commons.

Consequently, however strongly the king himself may be opposed to a change, he can but submit when the majority of the House of Commons has come to a decision in favor of it.

There had been a strong party in the House of Commons and in the country, opposed to the war from the beginning, and this party was gradually increased as the war went on, and the different European nations began to be drawn into it, or rather to avail themselves of the opportunity offered by it to advance their own claims and interests as against England, in various parts of the world. Of course every defeat of the British arms in America gave a great impulse to the opposition in Parliament, and tended greatly to discourage the friends of the party in power.

Effect of the Surrender of Cornwallis

The surrender of Cornwallis and his army took place about the middle of October, 1781, and the news of the event reached England toward the end of November, just before the opening of Parliament. It produced a great effect. A resolution was soon brought forward, declaring "That any further attempt to reduce the Americans by force would be ineffectual and injurious."

After an exciting debate the vote was taken. The ministry made great exertions to rally all their friends, and they succeeded in defeating the proposed resolution, though by a majority very much reduced from that of former votes on the question.

This was near the middle of December. The Christmas holidays came on soon afterward, when Parliament is always adjourned. During the interval it was evident that public opinion was moving rapidly in the direction of opposition to the war, and when Parliament assembled, after the recess, the question was brought up again, in the form of a proposed address to the king, requesting his majesty to put a stop to the war.

Notwithstanding all the influence which the ministry could bring to bear against this proposal, it was lost by only one vote.

A few days afterward it was brought forward again and carried.

The ministry were of course compelled to resign, that their places might be supplied by a new ministry opposed to the further prosecution of the war.

An Alternative Still Presented

This did not, however, entirely settle the question of independence; for of those who were opposed to the farther continuance of the war a considerable number still believed that by giving up the original point in dispute—that is, the claim of the Americans that their own legislatures should have the exclusive right to levy taxes upon them—just as the English legislature—that is, the Parliament—had the exclusive right to levy taxes upon the English people—and also by making other concessions, if desired, by which the colonies should hold practically the entire control of their local government—they might be induced to waive their demand for a formal and absolute separation from the mother country. It would of course greatly diminish the humiliation of England in giving up the contest if some semblance of union between the crown and the revolted provinces could be restored and maintained.

Attempt to Separate America from France

There was another point, which was likewise a kind of point of honor, or rather a question of pride, with the English statesmen in this emergency. The English government was very indignant against France for having interfered in a quarrel between the king of England and his own subjects, and for having aided and abetted them in their rebellion, especially as by so doing she had been in a great measure the means of enabling the traitors to accomplish their ends. And now, by consenting that France should be joined to America in the treaty of peace, they seemed to be in some measure recognizing and acknowledging, if not actually sanctioning, the alliance and union between them.

Besides this, it was in itself a very humiliating thing for a great sovereign to be compelled openly to allow a rival and hostile power to come in as a party to be consulted and satisfied, in the settlement of a quarrel between himself and his own subjects.

The English statesmen were accordingly very desirous of securing two points in the coming negotiations; first, to separate France entirely from America in the conduct of them, and secondly so to settle the quarrel as to retain some nominal connection still between the colonies and the mother country.

ATTEMPT TO NEGOTIATE WITH WASHINGTON AND CONGRESS

With a view perhaps of separating the American from the French government in the negotiations, and dealing only with the former, instructions were sent out to the general-in-chief of the British armies in America to open a communication on the subject of peace with Washington and with the Congress. Congress replied, however, that they had clothed the commissioners at Paris with full powers to act for the American government in the negotiations to be opened, and declined taking any action on the subject in any other way.

THE THREE ESSENTIALS

The British government finally sent a commissioner to Paris with powers to arrange with the American commissioners there the terms and conditions of a treaty. The name of the British agent was Oswald. He was not a member of the government, but a merchant of London, appointed by the ministry especially for this service. He at once proceeded to Paris in order to perform his duty. This was in the summer of 1782.

His instructions were to ascertain whether there was any possibility of arranging the settlement in such a way as still to preserve some connection between the colonies and the mother country; but he soon found that this was entirely out of the question. The commissioners declared that there were three essential conditions that must be agreed to before they would enter into any negotiations at all. Those three points were absolute independence, a satisfactory boundary, and a right to participation in the fisheries.

Finding the commissioners firm on these points, Oswald returned to London to report and to receive fresh instructions.

Technicalities and Points of Etiquette

After receiving these instructions Oswald went back again to Paris to renew the discussions. He arrived there early in September. On meeting the commissioners he produced his credentials in order that the commissioners might see that he was duly authorized to act. They observed that the language of the document was that he was empowered "to conclude a peace with *certain colonies.*"

Jay objected to this phraseology. The parties with whom the negotiation was to be made were not colonies, he urged, but independent states, having declared themselves such in 1776, six years before, and having maintained that declaration during the whole intervening period. For them to open negotiations as colonies, he contended, would he a virtual abandonment of the whole ground for which the battle had been fought, and that after the victory had been won.

Franklin, who was a man of plain practical common sense—accustomed to look at the substance rather than the form in all transactions in which he was engaged—while he admitted the force of this objection, was not inclined to insist upon it. He argued that though the British government might still use the word colonies, the very act of treating with them was in itself a recognition of their independence as a power; and that the objection to the technical informality might be waived. But Jay was a lawyer, and he knew very well how important in certain contingencies the legal effect of the language of the document might become.

He argued, furthermore, that the object of the treaty was not to *create* the independence of the American states nor even to procure an acknowledgment of it. The independence was a fact. The acknowledgment of that fact by the British government was to be the act of that government alone. No treaty was required for that. Indeed no treaty could be made until that act had been performed. Whether the British government would or would not recognize the fact of American independence was a preliminary question for the government alone to consider. If they decided that they could not recognize it, then no negotiations could be opened; for no government can negotiate or make treaties except with an acknowledged power. If, on the other hand, they decided that they did recognize the American government as an independent power, then the commissioners were ready to enter upon the negotiation of a treaty to define the relations which the two powers were to sustain to each other in their future intercourse; but it was obviously required, as a preliminary step, that the American government should be acknowledged as an independent power, capable of making such a contract, before the negotiation of it could be commenced.

These views prevailed and Oswald returned to London to obtain a change in the phraseology and tenor of his instructions.

True Character of the French Intervention

Although the Americans, as was very natural and very proper, felt a certain sense of obligation to their allies for the aid which they had rendered them in the war, it must not be supposed that the French were actuated in rendering this assistance, by any generous principle of justice, in behalf of the weak contending for their rights against the strong, still less from any sentiment of friendship or special goodwill for the American people. There is no such thing as generosity or friendship as a principle of action among nations— and no proper foundation for gratitude, such as is called for by disinterested kindness, or by favors bestowed without expectation of return. In all its dealings with the external world, every nation, as a nation, acts solely with a view to its own interests. Governments in fact have very little authority to act otherwise than with a single view to the advantage of their own people.

The aid which the French government gave to the Americans in the war of the revolution formed no exception to this general rule. Individuals may have been influenced by generous and self-sacrificing motives, but the government was led to the course it pursued solely by the desire to divide and diminish the power of its ancient and eternal rival and enemy, Great Britain.

They joined, accordingly, with the American government in the war, because by so doing they could the better accomplish certain objects of their own. The Americans were thus under just the same obligation to the French for aiding them to establish their independence that the French were to the Americans for the assistance that the revolution afforded them in humbling and weakening their ancient enemy.

Interference of French and American Interests in the Question of Peace

While the war continued the French and the Americans acted in harmony, for their interests and ends were the same. Both wished to inflict as much injury as possible upon the British military power, and to make the separation of the colonies from the mother country complete and perpetual. But when the terms and conditions of peace came to be discussed, the interests of the two governments were found to be very diverse. Each naturally wished to gain advantages for itself, and in order to accomplish this end endeavored to induce the other to be satisfied with little, in order that whatever of a spirit of concession the English government were disposed to evince, might be made available in obtaining for its own side the more.

The Western Boundary

There was a great deal of discussion during these negotiations in respect to the boundaries of the territory to be held by the United

States. The country between the Alleghenies and the Mississippi was then almost entirely uninhabited by white men, and the French and Spaniards who held large tracts of country south of the United States and west of the Mississippi, claimed that the country east of the river, as far as to the mountains, should not be included. To this, however, the commissioners would not consent. They insisted on the Mississippi as the western boundary.

THE FISHERIES

Another question related to the right of the Americans to a participation in the Newfoundland fisheries. The French minister endeavored to persuade the commissioners to give up this claim, and to be content with the fisheries on the coast. But to this the commissioners would by no means consent.

The Newfoundland fisheries were of great importance to the New England people, and especially to the people of Massachusetts. But besides this there was a national object to be obtained in retaining this branch of industry, and that was the securing for the country a large class of efficient seamen to be ready for the naval service in case of future wars.

DIPLOMACY

In diplomacy as in war, a great number of maneuvers and modes of management are practiced which are considered right and proper enough by the party that practices them, but which, when brought to light, are thought treacherous and dishonorable by the other party. The operation which those who are to gain by it consider only as adroit management, or ingenious stratagem, those who are to lose denounce as perfidy and fraud. There seems to have been a good deal of this kind of work among the various parties concerned in this complicated negotiation. There was secret correspondence carried on, and attempts made by each party to foment divisions and jealousies between the other two, and letters intercepted and shown to parties from whom they were intended to be concealed, and many other maneuvers of quite a questionable character. It is very natural for us, as Americans, to say that there was nothing of this kind in the conduct of our representatives in this transaction, and probably the French and the English would say the same in respect to theirs.

Claims of Compensation for the American Loyalists

The difficulties of the negotiation did not arise altogether from the claims made by the French and the Americans. The English on their part demanded some indemnification for the losses which the loyalists of New York, Boston and other large cities had sustained in consequence of the part they took against the colonies in the revolution. Some of these persons had had their property confiscated. Others had been obliged to fly precipitately from their homes, and had suffered great loss and damage.

Now most of the commissioners had taken a very active part in the measures which the different states had adopted against these loyalists during the whole period of the war, and were of course now extremely unwilling to engage that anything like restitution should be made to them for the damage they had suffered for having taken part against their countrymen. After much debate and much urgent insisting on both sides, the American commissioners finally agreed that there should be no farther proceedings taken against such of the loyalists as remained in the country, and that the general government should moreover recommend to the several states to restore the property which had already been confiscated, though they frankly admitted that Congress had no power to compel them to comply with the recommendation, nor did the commissioners think that there was much probability that they would comply with it of their own accord.

Terms of the Treaty Finally Agreed Upon

The principal points of the treaty, as it was finally arranged, were, that the independence of the thirteen states was formally and fully acknowledged, with the line of the St. Lawrence and the lakes for the Northern boundary, and the river Mississippi for the Western boundary, of the territory. The Americans were to have the free navigation of the Mississippi River, but the St. Lawrence was to be under the exclusive control of the English. Both nations were to have free access to the Newfoundland fishing ground.

Long Protraction of the Negotiations

The war virtually ceased when the negotiations were commenced, but it was a long time before the treaty was formally signed and ratified and the British troops actually withdrawn from the country. It was in the spring of 1782 that Parliament came to the decision to abandon the war. In the course of the summer of that year the negotiations were commenced in Paris. In November the preliminaries were agreed upon and signed, but the discussions that arose in drawing up the formal treaty occupied nearly a year longer, so that it was not until September, 1783, that the treaty was actually and finally signed.

Final Withdrawal of the British Army

The final evacuation of the country by the British troops took place a month later, from New York. The different portions of the army had previously been gradually concentrated at that point, and when the time arrived for their departure, the British general, Sir Guy Carleton, gave notice of their intended embarkation to General Washington, in order that he might be ready to take possession of the several posts in the vicinity of the city, and of the city itself, in succession, as the British troops should be withdrawn.

A conference was then held in the vicinity of the city between Sir Guy Carleton, General Washington, and Governor Clinton, the governor of New York, to arrange together the details of the evacuation. The twenty-fifth of November was fixed upon as the day.

The embarkation commenced at the appointed time, and as fast as the troops were withdrawn from the different posts, the forces of the Americans entered, took possession, and raised the national flag. When at last the city itself was left free, the Americans entered it, in a grand procession. General Washington and Governor Clinton led the way, escorted by a troop of horsemen. They were followed by a large number of other officers of rank, both civil and military, and by a long column of citizens on horseback and on foot.

In the evening the whole city was given up to festivities, military salutes, fireworks, illuminations, and general rejoicings. The last British soldier had gone and the country was at peace.

The anniversary of the evacuation continued to be celebrated by the inhabitants of New York for many years.

CHAPTER VI
THE DISBANDING OF THE ARMY

Resignation of Washington

As soon as the great object for which war had been organized and the armies raised—namely, the independence of the country—had been secured, Washington resigned his commission, thus divesting himself of the great military power which had been placed in his hands, and quietly retiring to private life. His doing this so promptly has justly been considered by mankind as an act which separates him by a marked line of distinction from all other heroes and conquerors that had in previous times, and in various ages of the world, succeeded in placing themselves at the head of the military power in their respective countries.

He alone of all the great commanders that have figured conspicuously in this world's history did not assume, when the battle was fought and the victory won, that he himself was the only man of all the millions interested who was capable of safely and successfully wielding the power which his military work had created. Julius Cæsar, Alexander, Charlemagne, the Napoleons—each, having established an empire, deemed it essential to secure the sovereignty of it to themselves and their descendants. Washington, as soon as his work of laying the foundation was done, and the existence and independence of the nation was secured, resigned his power into the hands of those who had conferred it, and retired.

The Nature of the Greatness of Washington

Washington was, as it were, the first of a new class of great men, such as the world before his day had scarcely known—that is, of men who acquire renown not by imposing their ideas and enforcing their will upon their countrymen, but by embodying and carrying into effect the ideas and determinations which their countrymen had previously formed. Washington did not originate the idea of the independence of America, as perhaps Julius Cæsar did that of the universal empire which he founded. The conception of American independence and nationality was gradually developed in the public opinion of a widely extended, intelligent, and well informed community. Washington was called upon to give effect to the will of this community, and for this purpose vast powers were put into his hands. When the work was accomplished he resigned the power, and returned to his retirement, leaving to that great community itself the entire responsibility of future action.

Assumptions of Other Founders of Empire

Other men who have been the means of founding empires have never pretended to be guided by the intelligence of any community, either in respect to the end to be attained or to the means of attaining it, but only to use its force as a means of attaining their own ends. They claim—or one of them, at least, claims for them—that when such men arise, and assume command over their fellow men, the nations whom they have succeeded in subjecting have only to listen to their voice and obey. Washington made no such claim, and assumed no such power. It was the voice of his country that was uttered, and he himself heard and obeyed.

The Soldiers

The dismission of the soldiers from the service was not so easily to be arranged, on account of difficulties arising from their arrears of pay, and other claims which they made against the government, and the unwillingness of the men to lay down their arms until their rights were secured to them. Several times during the war very serious complications had arisen from the inability of the government to fulfill its obligations to the men in respect to clothing, provisions, and pay. Mutinies leading to serious outbreaks several times occurred, and on one occasion a whole encampment of thirteen hundred men broke into open revolt, and after deposing the commissioned officers put the sergeants in their places, and set out on their march to Philadelphia, there to make a personal demand upon Congress for the redress of their grievances.

The Revolt in 1781

This occurrence took place in 1781, the year before the opening of negotiations for peace, and about six months before the capture of Cornwallis. The troops that were concerned in the revolt were those of Pennsylvania and New Jersey. They were encamped in winter quarters in Morristown, in the middle of New Jersey. Washington was at that time on the Hudson, a little above New York, to protect the country there, and the river, from the incursions of the British, who were in strong force in the city. In a word, it was during one of the most critical periods of the war that this difficulty occurred.

Causes of the Revolt

In respect to the questions at issue between the soldiers and the government, the mutineers, it would seem, were altogether in the right. The hardships, privations, and trials which they endured were pitiable in the extreme. Their clothes were worn to rags; their shoes were well-nigh gone; they were wholly unprovided with blankets or outside garments; and they had very little fuel for fires. The only means of protection from the cold that they could command was the shelter of wretched huts, which they built themselves, in cold and hunger. They had had no pay for months. In a word, they were reduced to the lowest extreme of destitution and misery that men could endure and live.

The officers did all in their power to sustain and encourage them, by sharing their exposures and fatigues, and they succeeded by these means, and by many strict precautions, in preventing an outbreak for some time.

The government declared that they had made, and were still making, every possible exertion to remedy these evils, but it was utterly out of their power to do it at once, though they made continual promises of relief soon to come. Their means, both of money and of credit, were entirely exhausted, and Congress knew not what to do to procure future supplies.

And yet the means and resources of the country were ample. For, during all this time, while the soldiers in camp were enduring these miseries, the cities, the large towns, and wide regions of fertile country were filled with hundreds of thousands of families, who, though suffering many inconveniences from the war, were still living at their homes in comfort and plenty, many of them enjoying all the refinements and pleasures of luxury and wealth. They remained at their homes and firesides unconcerned, while these poor outcasts put into the field to fight for their protection, were left to sink through all the successive stages of want and misery into utter despair.

WHY CONGRESS COULD NOT ACT EFFECTUALLY

The reason why Congress was powerless to redress this wrong, was because the period when the difficulty occurred was during the time of the confederation, when the general government could only decide what should be done, while they were wholly dependent upon the *states* for the means to do it. This difficulty was afterward remedied, as will be seen in a subsequent chapter, when the union was formed, under which the general government had not only authority to determine what should be done, but was clothed with power to carry its decrees into immediate execution by its own direct agency. Under the confederation, however, Congress could only decide, for example, that so much money or so many men should be raised, and then apportioning the amount among the several states, call upon each one to take measures for providing its share.

How this operated will be more fully shown hereafter. It is sufficient here to say that it led to endless difficulties, delays, and failures. Thus the men suffered because the concurrent action of fourteen independent powers was necessary for their relief, one to decide what was to be done, and the thirteen others to do it, by separate action—one by one—at times and in ways as should by them be found to be convenient and agreeable.

The Crisis

At length things were brought to a crisis in the encampment of the Pennsylvania troops above referred to, by a practical question which arose between the officers and many of the men, in which the officers felt bound to insist upon what the men considered an outrageous injustice. It seems that a large portion of the men had enlisted "for three years or during the war." It was not supposed at the time that the war would be protracted for more than three years, and the object of putting the contract in that form was to enable the government to disband the troops, and so terminate their pay, at any time when the war should end.

The three years had now expired with many of the men, and they, finding their privations and sufferings no longer endurable demanded their discharge. But the officers claimed that they were enlisted *for the war,* whatever its duration might be, and refused to grant any of them a discharge.

On this a large body of Pennsylvania troops made a common cause, and openly revolted. An actual conflict ensued, in which one man was killed and many wounded. The malcontents were however victorious, and as has already been said, they set out in a body on a march to Philadelphia to demand of Congress, in session there, at least a recognition of what they deemed their rights, and some redress for their intolerable grievances.

This was a terrible irruption upon the country intervening—a body of thirteen hundred armed men, breaking loose from the authority of their commanders, and from the discipline of the camp, and commencing a march of a hundred miles through a defenseless country, and all in a state of excitement and exasperation, under a sense of what they deemed outrageous wrong.

Danger and Difficulty of the Situation

The officer in command of the revolted troops, or rather the one who had been in command of them—General Wayne — immediately despatched couriers in every direction to give the alarm. He sent one to General Washington at his headquarters, on the Hudson River, near New York, to inform him of what had occurred, another to Philadelphia to give notice to Congress, and others to all the intervening country, with orders to spread the alarm everywhere by ringing the bells and building signal fires on all the heights, for the purpose of calling out the militia. This was done, partly in the hope of assembling a sufficient force to intercept the progress of the mutineers, and, if this should be impossible, to enable the country through which they should pass, to protect themselves from depredation and plunder. And in order to diminish as much as possible the danger of violence, and to remove from the men the temptation and excuse that hunger would afford them, General Wayne sent on a supply of provisions after them, sufficient for their wants on the way.

Washington's Danger

Washington's first impulse was to set off himself immediately in pursuit of the revolted troops, in hopes of overtaking them, and by his personal influence persuading them to return to their duty.

But his own situation and that of the army under his immediate command were such that it was not safe to do this. There was a degree of suffering and discontent among these troops scarcely less than that of the body which had revolted. If he were to leave them a revolt might break out among them also. They were, moreover, very near the British lines; and the British officers, on learning the true state of the case, might make such offers to the men as to induce them to give up the cause of their country entirely, and go over in a body to the enemy.

Endeavor of the British to Take Advantage of the Difficulty

The British general was, in fact, well apprised of what was taking place; and as soon as he was informed of the mutiny of the soldiers, and of their having commenced their march toward Philadelphia, he sent off at once several messengers to make their way through the country to the camp of the revolted troops, to offer them pardon, protection and ample pay if they would return to their allegiance to the king, and join his army.

At the same time he embarked with all haste, in the midst of a pouring rain, a number of pieces of artillery and a considerable body of men, with orders to the detachment to proceed along the Jersey shore, and to be ready to meet and receive the troops, if the messengers should succeed in persuading them to accept his offers, and to lead them down to the coast, where he would have transports ready to convey them to New York.

Measures Adopted by Washington

Immediately on receiving intelligence of the mutiny, and finding that it would not be safe for him to go personally to the scene, Washington sent orders to General Wayne to follow the men and endeavor to open friendly communication with them, but not to attempt any coercion. He was not even to attempt to surround them, or to intercept their march. If they found that they were in danger of being overpowered and captured, there would be great fear of their deserting in a body to the British. At any rate, they could not by any such course be ever made good soldiers again for the American cause.

The river Delaware, which forms the boundary between New Jersey and Pennsylvania, and which the mutineers would have to cross as soon as they reached the frontier of the state, would have afforded General Wayne a great facility in intercepting and capturing the mutineers if that had been the true policy to be pursued. But Washington's orders were that he should not attempt to prevent their crossing the river, but rather to facilitate their doing so, in order to remove them as far as possible from any aid that the British general might send to them. Washington at the same time sent communications to all the neighboring states—through whose remissness in carrying into effect the measures ordained by Congress this emergency had arisen—informing them of what had occurred and of the imminence of the danger which threatened and urging the legislative and executive authorities to comply with the requisitions of Congress without any further delay.

The Mutineers Come to a Stand at Princeton

The mutineers, however, did not seem disposed to hasten their march. On the contrary, after having proceeded to Princeton, a distance of about fifty miles from Morristown, and still fifteen or twenty from the river, they came to a halt and encamped. Here negotiations were commenced, and after considerable delay and much discussion terms were agreed upon by which the difficulty was settled.

Opening of the Conferences

When General Wayne overtook the mutineers at Princeton he found them regularly encamped, everything being arranged in order, and the men under the usual discipline. He himself and two of the officers accompanying him were admitted to the camp. The rest who came with him were excluded. General Wayne immediately opened a conference with the leaders in respect to their complaints and grievances, and to the means that he had at his command for remedying them.

Delegation from Congress

He was soon joined in these conferences by a delegation from Congress. For the Congress—then in session at Philadelphia—when the news was brought to them of the mutiny, had been greatly alarmed in view of the consequences that might ensue; and had immediately appointed a delegation to proceed at once to New Jersey, with a view of meeting the men on the way and holding a conference with them.

The committee of Congress, accompanied by President Reed, the chief executive of the state of Pennsylvania, and several other officers, and escorted, moreover, by a troop of horse, set off at once, and traveled with all dispatch toward the scene of danger.

The Emissaries from the British Army

In the meantime the emissaries which had been sent from the British general in New York, arrived at the camp, with their offers of food, clothing, protection and money to the men if they would come over to their side. The sergeants in command of the mutineers immediately seized these men and delivered them up, as spies, to General Wayne. They said that they, the mutineers, were not traitors, or deserters, and had no idea of abandoning the cause of their country, still less of going over to the enemy. They were not "Arnolds," they said—for the treason of Arnold had occurred not long before this time, and his name had already become a byword of reproach—but true men, ready still at any time to be led against the enemy. All that they were contending for was that while they were themselves faithful to their duty, they should not be subject to intolerable injustice and oppression from the government and the country.

The conduct of the men in seizing and delivering up the British agents tended very strongly to quiet the apprehensions and anxieties which the authorities had felt, and greatly facilitated the negotiations.

President Reed and the Delegation

It was necessary for President Reed and the congressional delegation to meet the men at a formal conference, in affecting the final settlement, and they were for a time quite uncertain about the expediency and safety of trusting themselves in their hands. A mutiny, whatever may be the apparent formality of its organization, is regarded by all regularly constituted authorities as a lawless mob, and no one could tell what excitements might suddenly break out among these men when they found prominent persons from among those against whom they had been so exasperated, in their hands, and at their mercy. In fact the delegation considered General Wayne and his two officers, though treated with apparent kindness and consideration, as really prisoners, and no one knew what would be their ultimate fate.

President Reed, however, though with many misgivings, decided to take the risk of putting himself in their power. He had but one life to lose, he said, and his country had the first claim to it.

President Reed took the most prominent part in the transaction, not only because he was the highest civil officer present at the time, but also because the troops in mutiny were chiefly those of the Pennsylvania line.

The Conference

At length, on a day appointed, President Reed with his suite of attendants, advanced to the camp of the mutineers, which was near the college at Princeton. They found guards posted at the entrances, and all the other observances of a regular military encampment in full force. The men were paraded in line, ready to receive their visitors with military honors. They were even prepared to fire a salute of artillery, having brought with them six pieces of cannon, but President Reed requested that this should not be done, for fear that the reports of the guns might create an alarm in the surrounding country.

It is not necessary here to detail all the particulars of the conference, but only to say that an agreement was made by which the demands of the men, which were after all only reasonable and just, were to be substantially complied with, that is, those who had enlisted for three years or the war, and who had reached the end of three years of service, were to be discharged, and proper arrangements were to be made in respect to the clothing and pay of the rest. The force was soon after marched forward to Trenton, where the promised arrangements were carried into effect, and the men returned to their duty.

The British Agents

The men who had been sent by the British general in New York to attempt to buy over the mutineers, were by the laws of war, spies. They were tried by a court-martial and hung at the crossroads near Trenton. In a moral point of view they had done nothing wrong, having only obeyed the command of their superior officer in coming within the enemy's lines, at the hazard of their lives, in hope of gaining a great advantage for the cause in which they were contending. But war does not look upon things at all from any moral point of view, but obeys the behests of military necessity alone; and military necessity requires that secret emissaries from the enemy, taken within any military camp, must die.

Rewards Offered for the Apprehension of the Spies

The mutineers, as has already been said, during their march and at their encampment at Princeton, were under the command of their sergeants, a grade of subordinate and non-commissioned officers, chosen from the men, and usually considered as specially sympathizing with them—not belonging themselves to the class of gentlemen officers. The spies, when they came and made themselves and their errand known, were arrested and delivered to General Wayne by two of these sergeants. After the difficulty was all settled, the authorities offered the sum of two hundred and fifty dollars each to these men, as a reward for their fidelity.

The men declined to receive the reward, saying that the act of arresting the men was not specially theirs. In making the arrest they only obeyed the orders of the whole board of sergeants, who directed everything. The amount of the reward then, five hundred dollars, was offered to the sergeants, collectively, in order that it might be divided among them.

They replied that in sending the spies to General Wayne they had not acted through any expectation of reward, but only from a sense of duty to the cause. They therefore, they added, did not consider themselves as entitled to any other recompense than the love of their country, and had jointly agreed not to accept of any other.

Just Estimation of the Conduct of the Mutineers

If common soldiers, or those who are in a social position to sympathize with them, were the writers of history, the action of the men in this mutiny would not only have been defended as justifiable and proper, but the whole transaction, considered in connection with all the circumstances that attended it, would have been conspicuously exhibited as one of the incidents of the war which show some of the noblest qualities of the American character, in a very striking point of view, and one consequently of which Americans have great reason to be proud.

But histories are written in general by those who are most in sympathy with the regularly constituted authorities, and such authorities can never admit that a mutiny is, under any circumstances whatever, other than a crime. Considering, however, the noble manner in which these men acted, and the calmness, prudence and moderation that they evinced in the measures which they adopted, none of those who have narrated the facts have had the heart to condemn the actors, and as they could not commend them, they have usually passed over the subject very briefly, using few words, and making fewer comments.

General Discontent of the Army toward the Close of the War

There were various other occasions on which the dissatisfaction of the soldiers produced serious difficulty during the course of the war, and the discontent and dissatisfaction which they felt became deeper and more general as the contest drew toward a close. For many months before peace was actually concluded, it was evident to all that the end of the war was drawing near. While therefore the troops were still kept together in the various camps, it was pretty certain that their active services would not be any longer needed, and this general conviction—though it ought not to have produced any such effect—did, in fact, greatly diminish the degree of urgency felt by the states, in regard to their obligation to comply with the requisitions of Congress for raising money to provide for immediate wants of the men, and for the arrearages of their pay.

General Washington's Remonstrances

General Washington often remonstrated against the injustice and the danger of this neglect. He wrote to Congress, to the governors of the states, and to leading men in all parts of the country, urging upon them the duty of providing the means of satisfying the just claims of the men before the time should arrive for disbanding them. Not only would it be ungenerous and unjust for the country to neglect this duty, but it would be highly dangerous to do so. He trembled, he said, for the consequences of sending forth so large a body of men, to be scattered through the community, all utterly destitute—half clothed, and without any means of reaching their homes except through the charity of the people on the way, and all in a state of great irritation and resentment against the government of their country, on account of the neglect and injustice with which they had been treated. If now, after exacting service from them for years, under circumstances of extreme exposure and suffering, in which they had undergone "all that human nature is capable of enduring this side of death," the government were to dismiss them without even making provision for the arrears of the slender wages which they had bound themselves to pay them, but leaving them far from their friends and homes, and without any means whatever of earning a livelihood, be thought that scenes of disorder and violence might ensue by which the peace of the country would be greatly disturbed.

SOME SMALL EXCUSE FOR THE INJUSTICE

It should somewhat diminish the pride and self-glorification with which the nation looks back at the present day to the grand and heroic action of their forefathers in the days of the revolution, that such a state of things as this could be allowed to exist. There is, however, some small excuse for the injustice of the country toward the men to whose services they owed so much, in the great difficulties of the situation, and the extreme imperfection and inefficiency of the governmental machinery by which the remedy was to be applied. The general government, it must be remembered, was then a confederation only, and Congress was only a species of commission with no power to act, except so far as the states should from time to time furnish them with the means. Congress could indeed determine what was to be done, but had no power to do it. It could not lay or collect taxes, nor in any other way carry into effect any of its decisions, except those relating to the actual operations of the armies in the field. In the case of money and supplies, they could only decide how much was required, and then apportion the amount among the several states, leaving the different legislatures to pass the necessary laws for raising their respective shares, and then to commission their local executives to carry these laws into effect.

The specific measures for carrying the requisitions of Congress into execution being thus referred to thirteen different legislatures, each of which was composed of men representing a great variety of conflicting interests, of course encountered innumerable difficulties and delays. Long debates were held in the several states, on the best mode of raising the tax, and on the proportions in which it should fall upon this or that article, or upon this or that class of the population. Whatever shape the law seemed about to assume, there were always many who wished to effect a change in it before it was passed, and they of course resorted to every means of protracting the debate, and procuring postponements and delays—their policy being aided, of course, by those who did not wish the money to be raised at all.

There were always some of this latter class. They did not openly avow any desire absolutely to refuse to pay the soldiers their due, but they wished the payment to be made in some other way than the one proposed. They, perhaps, charged the responsibility for the difficulty upon Congress. Congress had not managed affairs wisely. If they had done this thing, or had not done that, the emergency would not have occurred. Or the Congress ought to contrive some way of borrowing the money from capitalists, or by means of a loan negotiated abroad, so as to give the country time to recover a little from the effects of the war before heavy burdens of taxation were laid upon the people.

Thus there were endless excuses and causes of embarrassment and delay, which, operating upon such a number of different legislatures, put everything like combined and efficient action out of the question, and the poor soldiers were left to suffer.

The Proper Remedy

The obvious remedy was to reorganize the system in such a way as to confer upon the general government executive powers sufficient to enable it to carry into effect its ordinances and measures itself, by its own officers and agents, on a uniform system for the whole country, leaving the states to manage their own local affairs alone—that is to say, to change the confederation into a union so far as all national affairs were concerned, leaving it a confederation as before in respect to local affairs. This remedy was afterward applied, but the time for it had not yet come.

Special Exertions Made by Washington to Avert the Danger

Washington, in the meantime, did everything in his power to avert the threatening danger. He sent urgent representations to Congress and to the governors of the several states to induce them to press forward the adoption of the necessary measures without delay. His recommendations, and especially the statements of facts with which he enforced them, produced their effect, and something was done by means of which Washington could satisfy some of the more pressing wants of the men, and could also in some degree come to a settlement of their claims for arrearages, and give them pledges in respect to arrangements which were to be made for the future payment of them.

Furloughs

He also undertook cautiously to commence the process of dispersing the troops, by granting furloughs to all who desired it, and allowing them to go to their homes. Peace had not yet been made absolutely sure, and therefore it was not safe altogether to dismiss any considerable number of the men. But Washington deemed it safe to allow a portion of them to withdraw from the camps, subject to the power of the government to recall them if occasion should require. By this means the danger which might have attended the sudden disbanding of a large number of destitute and discontented men was greatly diminished.

Threatened Conspiracy among the Troops

The discontent and irritation of the soldiers seemed to arrive at its height in the spring. At this time hostilities had in a great measure ceased, and the main body of the army was encamped on the banks of the Hudson, a short distance above New York, while the British held the city, which, however, they were preparing to evacuate. Washington had his headquarters at Newburgh, fifty or sixty miles above the city.

The officers and soldiers of the army during the preceding winter had had little else to do than to reflect upon their position, and brood over the gloomy prospects that were before them, if they were to be discharged and sent to their homes in the destitute condition in which they found themselves likely to be placed. The officers in particular began to feel extremely uneasy. Many of them had been in service during the whole period of the war. Those whose health had not been seriously impaired by the diseases of the camp had become prematurely old and infirm through exposure and suffering. They had expended not only the little pay which they had received, but also their own private means, and they had become disqualified for earning a livelihood by any of the ordinary occupations of civil life. After having spent the flower of their days in toil and suffering to protect the rights of millions of people against a very determined foe, and to lay the foundation of a great and independent government, and having fully succeeded in their work, they saw nothing before them for the remainder of their days but to live the life of wretched outcasts, in poverty and shame, and dependent on charity even for their daily bread—while the great people whom they had been the instruments of redeeming went on triumphantly in the career of prosperity and wealth which was opening before them.

Anonymous Addresses Circulated in Camp

While things were in this state, a great excitement was produced by several anonymous addresses which were circulated among the officers in Washington's camp, calling upon them to form a combination for the assertion of their rights, and for forcing the government, if necessary, to do them justice. The addresses represented in very earnest and vigorous language the terribly humiliating and destitute condition to which the officers and soldiers would be reduced, if they allowed themselves to be disarmed and disbanded before proper provision was made by the government for fulfilling its obligations to them; and it called upon them not to submit to this wrong. The course which these communications proposed as the proper one to be pursued was first to address the government in the most firm and decided manner, demanding their rights, and then if their demand should not be complied with, to refuse to give up their arms, but to put their beloved chief, meaning Washington, at their head, and take the means of redress into their own hands.

Many cases have occurred in history where the leaders of a great army, the foremost among them at the head, have at the close of a long war, retained their arms and organization, overturned the civil government, and established a military one in its stead. Julius Cæsar and the first Napoleon are two conspicuous examples of this mode of instating a military leader in supreme and irresponsible power, and Washington might have at least attempted to make himself a third, if he had been so disposed.

Conduct of Washington in the Emergency

He was, however, not so disposed. Instead of taking advantage of the occasion to make himself an emperor, he devoted all his powers and all his influence, both with the army on one side, and with Congress, the different state legislatures, and the country on the other, to heal the breach. He came before the officers in a meeting which they held to take these proposals into consideration, and there made an address to them, expressing principles so exalted and noble, combined with sentiments of the strongest personal attachment to them, as the beloved comrades who had been joined with him in so long and arduous a work, and had endured with him so many sufferings—while at the same time he evinced a just sense of the wrongs which they had endured, and explained the measures which he was adopting to secure redress for them by proper and legitimate modes, that the angry feelings of the men assembled were greatly soothed, and the danger of an open insurrection of the army against the government was averted.

He also wrote new and more earnest letters to Congress, and to the governors of the states, representing the danger of the crisis, and the justice of the demands made by the army, in such a light that new efforts were made, and before long the claims of the men were substantially satisfied, and the way was prepared for the peaceable dispersion of the troops when the time at length arrived.

Washington's Farewell to the Army

The occasion, however, of Washington's farewell to his troops preparatory to their final separation, was a very sad and sorrowful one, for besides the pain of parting from one whom the men had always looked up to as a father, their prospects for the future, notwithstanding all that had been done for them by Congress, including the engagements yet to be fulfilled, were very dark and gloomy. They bade each other and their beloved general farewell in much sorrow and with many anxious forebodings, and went forth into the wide world where many of them had no friends and no home—and no visible means of future subsistence—with hearts full of despondency and gloom.

Washington's Parting with His Officers

The final parting of Washington from his principal officers, was, if possible, still more affecting. The interview took place in New York a few days after the British troops had evacuated the city, and the American authorities had been put in possession. Washington remained in town two or three days, for the purpose of bringing his military duties to a close, and also of joining in certain festivities proposed by some of the principal inhabitants.

When the appointed day arrived, a barge, elegantly fitted up, was prepared to convey him across the Hudson River to the Jersey shore, that he might proceed to Philadelphia, with a view of settling his accounts with the department of war there, and then formally resigning his commission. The barge was stationed at Whitehall, near the battery, and a military escort was provided to attend him through the street.

The officers met to take their leave of him at the hotel where he lodged. When they were all assembled he was introduced into the room. He went to a sideboard, poured out a glass of wine, and as he raised it to his lips in presence of them all—though so much moved that it was difficult for him to utter the words—he said to them that the time for their parting had come, and that it was with a heart full of love and gratitude that he took leave of them—adding the wish that their future days might be as prosperous and happy as their previous ones had been honorable and glorious.

Then, bowing, he touched the glass to his lips, in token of drinking to the health and happiness of his friends.

He then said that he could not conveniently come to take them severally by the hand, the room being very full; but he wished that each one of them would come to him. This they did; and the parting salutation was given in this way, accompanied by inarticulate expressions of goodwill, and many tears.

Washington then immediately left the hotel, and, followed by a long procession, he walked in silence to Whitehall, where the barge was awaiting him. It was then about two o'clock. As the barge left the pier Washington turned toward the people that crowded in throngs upon the shore, and taking off his hat waved to them his farewell.

Settlement of the Accounts

Washington proceeded on his journey across the state of New Jersey. The people thronged the towns and villages through which he passed, and received him everywhere with joyful acclamations. He arrived at length at Philadelphia, and remained there for a few days to present and settle his accounts in the proper offices. These accounts included only charges for actual expenses incurred by him during the war. Except this reimbursement for actual outlay, he would accept no remuneration for the services that he had rendered.

Final Resignation

Having closed this business, he proceeded to Annapolis, where Congress was then in session, in order to render back his commission into the hands of those who had conferred it, thus formally resigning his command and divesting himself entirely of all power. He had intended to have sent in the commission, accompanied by a written communication, instead of surrendering it in person; but Congress desired that the ceremony should be performed in a more formal and solemn manner. They were probably aware that this act of quietly resigning his power into the hands of the civil authorities that had conferred it, when the object for which it had been conferred had been accomplished, was one which would be recognized by mankind as the crowning glory of the hero's life, and one which would forever distinguish him in the estimation of the world from all previous conquerors and founders of empires, of whatever country or age.

The Ceremony

At the appointed time, which was at twelve o'clock on the 20th of December, 1783, the hall of Congress was filled, the members occupying their seats in the center, while all the other available space on the floor and in the galleries was crowded with ladies, public officers, and other such persons of distinction as had been able to obtain admission. Washington was then introduced, and conducted to a chair which had been placed for him in a central position. As soon as silence was restored he rose with his commission in his hand, and made a brief address to the president.

> "The great events," he said, "on which my resignation depended having at length taken place, I have now the honor to offer my sincere congratulations to Congress, and of presenting myself before them, to surrender into their hands the trust committed to me, and to claim the indulgence of retiring from the service of my country."

Then, after speaking a few words in strong commendation of the officers and soldiers that had served under his command, and earnestly commending them to the favor of Congress and to the gratitude of the country, he concluded by saying:

> "I consider it an indispensable duty to close this last solemn act of my official life by commending the interests

of our dearest country to the protection of Almighty God, and those who have the superintendence of them to his holy keeping.

"And having now finished the work assigned me, I retire from the great theater of action; and bidding an affectionate farewell to this august body, under whose orders I have long acted, I here offer my commission and take my leave of all the employments of public life."

As he said these words he delivered his commission into the hands of the president, who, on receiving it, made a brief but very touching address to Washington in reply.

Those who witnessed the scene recorded the fact that the whole audience were entirely overcome by the emotions which it awakened in their minds.

Return to Mount Vernon

On the following day, the twenty-first, Washington set out on his return to his home in Virginia. The journey occupied several days on account of the great desire of the people to see him on the way, and the many interruptions to his progress occasioned by the requests made to him, at the different towns which he passed through, that he would stop to receive addresses from the authorities, and to take part in ceremonies of welcome and congratulation. He arrived at Mount Vernon on Christmas Eve, just in time to join in the grand festivities by which that occasion is always marked on every southern plantation, and which were redoubled in this case by the excessive delight experienced by all on the estate in seeing again their long absent chieftain, and welcoming him once more to his home.

CHAPTER VII
THE CONFEDERATION

Three Successive Forms of Combination Adopted by the States

The states now constituting the American republic have combined for united action under three distinct organic forms, in three successive periods, namely, that of the Continental Congress, of the Confederation, and of the Union. The Continental Congress continued in power for six years, namely, from 1775 to 1781—the confederation for eight years, namely from 1781 to 1789—and the Union for more than half a century, up to the present time; and there is now every indication that with such modifications as it may make upon itself from time to time, by its own internal action, it will endure as long as any existing human institutions.

Essential Difference in the Nature of These Systems

The Continental Congress was essentially only an advisory body. It consisted of delegates appointed in various ways by the several colonies, to consult and advise, but with no formal power to act, except in the conduct of military operations. The Congress assumed to speak in the name of all the colonies, and to recommend to them severally what it was best to do; but it had no authority really to decide any question, still less any power to carry such decisions into effect. Under the confederation on the other hand—which was the second form of combination—the general government was clothed with certain powers to decide finally the questions coming before them, and to pass enactments binding on the states, but they had no power to carry their measures into effect. This was to be left to the states themselves. The Congress decided what money should be raised, and what number of men furnished, but then the actual raising of the men, and the collecting of the money was to be left to the state authorities alone, according to the quotas which Congress should assign to them respectively. In other words the states reserved to themselves all real power, but, in relation to national subjects, they bound themselves by a solemn compact to exercise their power in accordance with the decrees of the delegates representing them, in Congress assembled.

Under this system, though there could be unity of plan, and in theory a certain unity of authority, there could be no real unity of action.

The country, however, succeeded in struggling through the period of the war under this system, though the difficulties and embarrassments encountered in the working of it were at times nearly fatal to the cause.

NATURE OF A CONFEDERATION

This system was, as its name imports, a confederation, that is a leaguing together of separate and independent governments, none of them surrendering any of their powers, but only agreeing to exercise their powers in respect to certain specified subjects, as should be determined upon by mutual agreement.

THE UNION

The third plan was a Union—that is a giving up by the states a portion of their governmental power, in order that the people of the country might mingle and blend themselves into one great community, in respect to all common and national purposes, while for all local purposes the states remained independent and sovereign as before.

Thus, under the first system the organ of the combination—the Congress—could speak and recommend, but could not decide or act. Under the second it could decide, but could only act through the agency of the state governments. Under the third it could not only decide, but was provided with all the requisite machinery and power for carrying its decisions and its measures into effect, within its own proper sphere, without consulting or calling upon the state governments at all.

Duration of the Continental Congress

Although when the serious work of the war came on, the Continental Congress system was found to be wholly inefficient for the accomplishment of the purposes required, it was undoubtedly at the time of its adoption the wisest, and in fact the only mode of cooperation that was possible. It continued to fulfill its functions, as has already been said, until the year 1781, that is for a space of six years, and did not cease to exist until it had itself produced its successor, the confederation, as that in its turn produced the Union, the last, and perfect form, which we hope will be perpetual.

First Movement in Favor of a Confederation

The total inadequacy of the powers of the Continental Congress for the exigencies of the situation was perceived at once, and measures were commenced almost immediately to establish some system that should be more worthy of the name of a government. In 1776, soon after the Declaration of Independence was made, a committee was appointed to draw up articles of confederation. In about a month the committee reported a plan.

Debates on the Subject in the Continental Congress

The subject was, however, so vast, so numberless were the forms which such a league might assume, so various were the conceptions and desires of the different members, arising partly from fundamental differences in their ideas of the nature of government, and partly from the diverse, and in some cases conflicting, interests of the different sections of country, that months passed away in discussing the various plans and projects brought forward in place of the one proposed by the committee, and in offering and debating innumerable amendments.

Of course it was but a small portion of the time occupied by its sessions that Congress could devote to this business, their attention being mainly engrossed by the immediate and pressing demands made upon them by the emergencies of the war. For during all this time, while they were engaged in the endeavor to construct some foundation of authority for their action, in a covenant among the states, they were obliged to act as it were without authority in carrying forward the work of the revolution.

Articles of Confederation Adopted and Proposed to the States

It was not until November, 1777—more than a year after the subject was first brought forward in Congress—that a plan of confederation was finally agreed upon, to be proposed to the states. Of course, it was necessary that it should be unanimously agreed to by them before it could be binding; or, at least, it could only bind those who should thus assent to it. For this was an *original* compact, and no one state could be rightfully compelled by the others to come into it against its will.

A confederation or constitution once made and formally agreed to, which contains *within itself* a provision for making alterations and amendments by a specified majority, may of course afterward be so amended by that majority; and the minority, having previously agreed to the compact, the provision for amendments included, will be bound by the decision. But the original compact, binding states previously entirely distinct and independent, can of course bind only those who voluntarily adopt it.

Provisions of the Proposed Confederation

The essential feature of the confederation was that the states bound themselves by a solemn league with each other that they, the states, would maintain and carry into effect whatever decisions the Congress, acting equally for all should decide upon, in relation to certain business of common interest—principally questions of peace and war, and those of commercial intercourse with foreign nations.

Under the Union, subsequently created, the general government was clothed with power to maintain and carry into effect its measures *itself*, without calling upon the state governments at all, and this constituted the essential difference between the two systems.

Thus under the confederation, Congress was to decide, when any question should arise with any foreign nation, whether war should be made, and, if made, they were to notify to each state what its proportion was of the men and money required for the proper conduct of the military operations, and the states, on receiving this notification, were bound to raise their respective quotas. It was the same with all the other undertakings which Congress might ordain. And as a government can do nothing at all without men and money, wherever the control over these supplies is placed there lies the real power. Under the confederation this power was left wholly in the hands of states.

The states positively bound themselves, it is true, by their agreement to furnish the supplies when Congress called upon them to do it; but, in case of their refusal or neglect to respond, there were no means of compelling them to do so.

Majority Required

Nor were they bound to furnish the means of carrying into effect any measure resolved upon by Congress unless there was a majority of *nine* states in favor of it. The number of states being thirteen, a simple majority would have been seven. But a majority of nine to four was required before any state could be called upon to act. This provision was intended to render it certain that the case was clear and decided before Congress could engage in any enterprise involving the country in expense, or committing it to any new course of foreign policy.

The States Equal under the Confederation

Each state being regarded as entirely sovereign and independent, and the national council being simply a league formed among them, no distinction was to be made among them, in respect to their voice in the council, on account of differences of wealth, of territory, or of population. Any of them might, if it chose, send several delegates—any number from three to seven; but in taking votes each state was to be counted as one.

And yet in raising men and money the different states were required to furnish their respective quotas in proportion to the value of the real estate comprised within its limits.

This plan of giving all the states, large and small, the same power in determining upon the measures to be adopted, while the large ones were to furnish far the greater portion of the means required for carrying the measures into effect, was very seriously objected to by the larger states, who thought that their voice in the decision ought to bear some proportion to the share of the burden which the decision imposed. But the smaller states thought that it would be entirely inconsistent with their dignity as sovereign and independent powers to join a league under any other terms than absolute equality in the council with the rest, both in consideration and in power.

This question was not easily settled. It led to much dissension and debate among the states when the articles were presented to them for ratification, and it caused a long delay on the part of many of them before they would yield their final assent to the plan.

No Executive Department

There was, strictly speaking, no executive department under this system, inasmuch as all the actual authority of government over individual citizens, was reserved by the states in their own hands. The general government had no immediate access at all to the individual citizen. It had only to direct the employment of such supplies of men and money as the states should furnish it. There was, of course, no chief magistrate to be elected, no cabinet of ministers, or other machinery of a central government. Provision was made for the appointment of a committee to act in the place of Congress, during the intervals of the sessions, but so jealous were the people at that time of the rights of the individual states, that it was provided by the articles that this committee should consist of one member from each state, so that even in the committee all the members of the league should stand upon an equal footing.

Common Citizenship

The foregoing were the great essential principles of the confederation. There were a number of subordinate provisions, tending to produce harmony and goodwill among the people of the States, and to facilitate social and commercial intercourse among them. The people of each state were to have free access and egress to and from any other one, and no distinctions of any kind were to be made, by the laws or ordinances of any state, between its own citizens and those of the other members of the Confederacy.

And if any person guilty of crime were to escape from one state to another, he was not to be harbored and protected, but to be arrested and given up, to be tried in the state where the crime was alleged to have been committed.

Restrictions on Separate State Sovereignty

By the proposed articles the several states bound themselves not to make war individually on any foreign power, nor even to hold any diplomatic intercourse with foreign nations, but in all cases to act on such questions in concurrence with the other states through Congress. They also agreed not to make any partial leagues or agreements with other nations, of any kind whatever. And no state was to own any vessels of war, or to organize and retain any armed force, except so far as authorized so to do by the action of Congress.

Provision for the Settlement of Questions of Controversy Arising between One State and Another

To prevent all possibility of any interruption to the internal interests of the country by hostilities between one state and another, systematic provision was made for the settlement of any question which might arise among them, by boards of referees, or temporary tribunals, appointed under the general direction of Congress, by the parties themselves if they could agree, and if not by a system of selection, by the disputants, or by lot, or by the two methods combined. No permanent judicial tribunal was included in the plan.

Thus it will be seen by a general survey of the system that it was substantially a plan for dividing the governmental power of the country into two great branches, all power of communication with the external world and all action in reference to it, being committed to the sole management and direction of the general government, the several states agreeing, each in its own way and in its own proportion, to carry into effect such decisions as the general government should make; while authority of every kind over individual citizens and local interests, and all the internal machinery of government, was retained exclusively in the hands of the states themselves.

THE ARTICLES OF CONFEDERATION ADOPTED BY CONGRESS AND TRANSMITTED TO THE STATES

It was not until the fall of 1777, that the articles were finally adopted by Congress, and ordered to be transmitted to the several states for their ratification. The states were very slow in giving their sanction to the plan. And of course, as it was extremely desirable that all the states should be included in any arrangement that should be made, and as no one could be included in it except by its own express consent, it became almost absolutely necessary to wait for an unanimous ratification before the system could go into effect. More than four years elapsed before this unanimous consent was obtained. The state of Maryland was the last to yield. Her adhesion was given in March, 1781, and on the following day Congress assembled under the confederation as the organic law of the union.

LITTLE ADVANTAGE GAINED

No very serious inconvenience, however, resulted from the delay; for, after all, the condition of the government seems not to have been much changed by the adoption of the articles—the Congress having exercised before, by the tacit acquiescence and consent of the states, pretty nearly the same powers with those conferred now upon it under the confederation, by a written instrument in a formal manner. Under the former system Congress could decide upon the measures to be adopted, and carry them into effect so far as the states severally by their voluntary action gave them the means. The Confederate Congress could decide more authoritatively, it is true, and could *require* the states to furnish them the means to carry their measures into effect. But still all depended now as before upon the voluntary action of the states, for they were at liberty to comply or not to comply with the requisitions made upon them, since there was nowhere any provision made for enforcing compliance.

During the remainder of the war, therefore, and for some time after hostilities were concluded, the government of the country moved slowly on, weak and inefficient in its action, holding a nominal authority over the direction of public affairs, but having no power to provide itself with the means of carrying its decisions into effect.

INFLUENCE OF PEACE AND WAR IN RESPECT TO THE OPERATION OF THE AMERICAN SYSTEM OF GOVERNMENT

As soon as the war was over, and the army was disbanded, the machinery of the confederation seemed to become more weak and its powers more insignificant than ever. It will probably always be a characteristic of our compound system of government—a general government chiefly for external, and local ones for internal, affairs—that the relative importance and prominence of the two branches of power will depend very much upon the condition of the country, whether it be in peace or in war. In time of peace and of quiet industry the state governments will as it were occupy the chief field of duty, while in time of war the general government will at once assume new importance, and often perhaps appear to usurp new powers, whereas it in fact only calls into exercise those that are perfectly legitimate, though previously dormant and held in reserve.

It has been strikingly so in the great rebellion, now in 1865 happily ended. One ostensible ground of the rebellion was to preserve the rights of the states, and diminish the power and prestige of the general government. The effect of the outbreak was at once to develop in the general government, by the natural and normal working of the system, a gigantic power fully adequate to the emergency, and in presence of which the state governments are comparatively silent and inactive. When, however, at length, the rebellion is ended, and an era of peace and quiet industry returns, the general government subsides into its ordinary channels. Its vast armies are disbanded, its fleets of ships and transports are dispersed, a large portion of its forts are dismantled, and its acts and operations have less power to monopolize and absorb public attention, while the functions of the state governments resume their wonted predominance in the thoughts and daily avocations of the citizens.

TERMINATION OF THE REVOLUTIONARY WAR

The termination of the revolutionary war produced this effect in a remarkable degree upon the old government of the confederation. It had, in fact, scarcely any life in itself, and was mainly kept in existence by the external pressure of difficulty and danger. As soon as this pressure was removed, all interest in the general government appeared rapidly to subside. The chief thing that then remained for Congress was the duty of providing ways and means for paying debts—always an irksome and disagreeable task. It was still more irksome and disagreeable in this case as the body charged with it had no real power to do the thing required, but only to determine in what proportions the several states should do it.

It was a long time before even a quorum to transact business could be secured. It was provided by the articles that nine states must be represented in order to constitute a quorum. Now, each state was to pay the salary of its own delegates. They naturally wished to save this expense. So they allowed small obstructions to prevent or delay the appointment of delegates. The duties to be performed, too, were irksome, and were attended with responsibility without power. This caused it to be very little an object of desire on the part of statesmen to be chosen. The consequence was that for some time no business could be done, because no Congress could be assembled.

RESIGNATION OF THE SECRETARY OF THE TREASURY

The Secretary of the Treasury, after struggling for a year or more against the insurmountable difficulties of his work, resigned his position, and no competent man could be found to take his place. Congress was obliged to appoint a committee to take charge of the financial affairs of the government. There was, however, very little that such a committee could do. Debts were pressing, and even interest money was falling fast in arrear; but the supply of funds coming in was extremely small, and there seemed to be no conceivable means of increasing it. In a word, the financial condition of the government was fast becoming desperate.

The Army

Even the physical force at the command of the general government rapidly dwindled away till it reached almost the vanishing point. There were only about seven hundred men reserved in the service when the army was disbanded, and this number had gradually diminished, until at length only about fifty men in one place and twenty-five in another, were left to guard certain magazines. And this was the military establishment of what had been organized as a mighty nation.

State of Completely Suspended Animation Reached at Last

Whatever of vital power had been imparted to the system at first went on in this manner, wasting gradually away, until at length at one time, all life seemed to be extinct, and the government, so far as any visible or tangible embodiment of its authority was concerned, entirely ceased to exist. It will be remembered that provision had been made for the appointment of a committee of one from each state to act as a kind of executive board during the adjournment of Congress. Such a committee was appointed. But in attempting to transact the business committed to them, they soon came to a hopeless state of disagreement, and the two parties into which they were divided were so nearly equal that all action was paralyzed. The members of the committee finally separated and went to their homes, leaving the government without any representation whatever.

Subjects Demanding Attention from the General Government during These Times

And, though the interests depending upon the action of the general government were much less important now than during the continuance of the war, there were very important interests at stake, which required some efficient agency to attend to them. There were negotiations to be carried on with foreign powers, not only with a view to arranging treaties of commerce, which now became quite necessary, but also to determine certain questions relating to boundaries and other subjects that were not yet settled, and which threatened to lead to serious consequences if not soon arranged. There were questions at issue with Spain, in respect to the navigation of the Mississippi, which passed near its mouth through what was then Spanish territory. The English, too, were very slow in giving up possession of some of the western forts, claiming that some of the obligations on our part, created by the treaty made with her, had not been fulfilled. There were difficulties moreover, in respect to certain Indian tribes, and a system of policy to be framed and determined upon as the future policy of the country in dealing with them. There were also a great many perplexing questions in regard to the disposal of vast tracts of public land, which had belonged to the several states, but which it was now proposed should be ceded to the general government, to be held under their jurisdiction as territories, with a view to their ultimate settlement and formation into states to be joined to the confederation.

General Conviction of the Necessity that a Stronger Government Should be Established

These questions, though all important, were not of such immediate and pressing urgency as to force the country to supply, by an outside pressure upon the Confederate government, the necessary stimulus to bring its feeble and waning vitality into action. Indeed, the conviction was gradually extending that some very different system of national combination than that then existing, under which the general government had no power to supply itself with the means of acting—but was wholly dependent on the concurrent action of thirteen different and independent sovereignties to supply them, was indispensably required. This feeling gradually extended itself through the community for several years, and different statesmen of eminence were turning their thoughts toward the nature of the change which it would be necessary soon to make, when certain events occurred which greatly tended to hasten this determination. These events were riots and disturbances which broke out in different parts of the country, and which the state authorities found themselves incompetent to manage. The most serious of these disturbances took place in the heart of Massachusetts, and is known in history as Shay's insurrection.

Shay's Insurrection

The causes of all these disturbances were substantially the same. They arose from the general exhaustion of the country after the long war, the poverty of the mass of the people, the pressure of debt, the scarcity of money, and the harassing operation of the legal processes by which the payment of debts was enforced. All this time there were many persons in the great cities, living in wealth and luxury, some of whom had made their fortunes in some way or other out of the war, and others by the lucky commercial ventures for which such stormy times always afforded many occasions to shrewd businessmen living in the great commercial centers. The officers of the state government, too, received handsome salaries, which the people in their destitution were taxed very heavily to pay. The professional men also charged high fees, and both these classes and the wealthy people generally, especially in the large towns, affected in their mode of living a good deal of the aristocratic state and display which English usages had long since introduced into the country.

It is not surprising that under these circumstances many of the people considered themselves aggrieved. They attributed their distress to the action of the government, and especially to the harshness of the measures for collecting debts. There were a great number of men in the interior of Massachusetts who were under this excitement, and a certain Captain Daniel Shays, who had been an officer in the revolutionary army, and had there acquired some military experience and skill, put himself at the head of them. He called them together at Worcester, and organized them into quite a regular army, which embodied at one time a force of about a thousand men. The immediate objects of the insurgents, so far as they appeared to have formed any definite designs, were to prevent the session of the courts in Worcester and Springfield, and also—with a view to ulterior operations—to get possession of the arms in the arsenal at Springfield.

The General Government Powerless

Of course this state of things produced general alarm throughout the country, and the general government was at once looked to as the source from which the required help was to be obtained. Now the general government had power to send troops to the scene of danger, provided it only had troops to send. But it had no troops. It could obtain troops easily if it had money. But it had no money. It could have borrowed money easily if it had the power to lay and collect taxes to pay it. But it had no such power. It could only engage with the capitalists to whom it applied for a loan, that it would *require* the several states to lay such taxes—each for its own fair proportion of the debt; but this was not likely to be considered by the capitalists who were to furnish the money as very satisfactory security.

It was, however, at length ascertained that some wealthy men in Boston, alarmed probably by the danger to themselves and to their property, threatened by the outbreak, offered to take the risk of furnishing the money to the general government, but before the arrangement could be completed and an army raised, the insurrection broke out in full force, and the authorities of Massachusetts were left to deal with it alone.

The Insurrection Subdued

The governor of Massachusetts called out the militia, and a force of four thousand men was put under the command of General Lincoln. This force moved at once into the disturbed district, and something like a civil war raged in the interior of Massachusetts for many weeks. All hope of any aid from the general government seems to have been abandoned, and Massachusetts called, instead, upon the neighboring states for their aid. This aid was readily furnished, and by means of great firmness and decision in the adoption of the necessary measures, and great moderation and forbearance in the execution of them, the insurgents were finally captured or dispersed, with few actual conflicts, and comparatively little loss of life.

Many of the leaders were taken, tried and condemned to death, but they were not executed. Indeed so good ground had they for their complaints, and so severe had been the hardships and sufferings that had led them to this desperate mode of redress, that it was estimated that one-third of the people of the state believed that they were justified in taking up arms.

All Confidence in the Confederate Government Finally Lost

One of the most important results of Shay's insurrection was completely to convince the country of the total inadequacy of the system of the government which had been adopted for the purposes in view. If, in the case of a dangerous insurrection breaking out in the heart of the country, the general government proved utterly helpless, so that the state whose peace was broken must be left to her own resources, and to such voluntary aid as she could obtain by calling upon her neighbors in her distress, what possible reliance could be placed upon it in any time to come? It soon appeared that all respect for so frail and feeble a system was gone, and demands began to arise from all parts of the country for the calling of a general convention to devise a more efficient plan of organization.

At length delegates to such a convention were appointed by all the states. The time for the meeting of it was the fourteenth of May, 1787, about three years after the close of the revolutionary war.

During all this time Washington had remained quietly at his home at Mount Vernon, taking comparatively little part in the management of public affairs. He was, however, now appointed by the state of Virginia as one of the delegates to the new convention.

CHAPTER VIII
THE UNION

Origin of the Convention

Although Washington took no prominent part in the management of public affairs immediately after the close of the war, and during the continuance of the confederation, the origin of the actual convention which formed the federal constitution is traced to his agency. While living in retirement at Mount Vernon, his mind was naturally turned to the condition of his native state, and to plans of improvement which might promote her welfare. Among other plans, he conceived the idea of improving the navigation of the Potomac, and perhaps connecting that river with the Ohio, by a canal. This plan would require the concurrent action of several states, and he took measures for having delegates appointed from the states interested, to meet at Mount Vernon in order to consider the subject. In discussing the plan proposed, the delegates were naturally led to the consideration of other plans connected with, or in some way bearing upon the project of the canal, and affecting a still greater number of states; and this turned their thoughts to the great necessity there was of a general government of the country that should be invested with some substantial power, by means of which national interests of this kind might be provided for in a regular and proper manner. The discussions arising in this way led to a gradual enlargement of the ideas of those who took part in them, until at length all partial schemes were abandoned, and it was finally determined that application should be made to Congress to call a general convention of all the states, to devise and recommend such changes in the articles of confederation as should give the country an efficient general government.

Difficulties in the Way

The difficulties in the way of the accomplishment of any such scheme were enormous, and might well have been considered by those who projected it, as absolutely insurmountable. It is plain that no power could be granted to the general government, except such as should be taken away for this purpose from the several states. Now each of the states considered itself, as it really was, independent and supreme in the management of its affairs, and each attached great importance to its supremacy. They had been allied together, it is true, in a war against a common foe, but there had been hitherto no other bond to unite them. The Confederate Congress had indeed continued feebly to fulfill its functions since the war was closed, but its duty had been chiefly confined to the adjustment of the accounts connected with the war, that still remained unsettled, and notifying the several states of the amounts which they were respectively called upon to pay, from time to time, in order to bring the business to a close.

Thus what we now call the general government of the country, at that time was not in fact, and was not then regarded, as a government at all—but only a confederation of governments exercising power through a kind of board of commissioners appointed to manage the affairs of thirteen allied states during the time of war, and continued in office after the war was closed, mainly for the purpose of settling up its affairs. The only real governments were the governments of the states.

Great Importance Attached to the Idea of State Sovereignty

Now the people were everywhere extremely tenacious of this idea of the sovereignty and independence of the states. The idea of a general nationality had not yet been formed in any minds, and such an idea cannot at once be created by conventions and constitutions. The several states had been settled in very different ways; the character of the people inhabiting them was very diverse; their ideas, their conceptions of the nature of government, and all their social usages were extremely various. Then there was none of that universal intercourse and intercommunication which exists at the present day to make the people of different regions acquainted with each other, and to mix and blend their ideas and opinions. There were not only no railroads, but not even stagecoaches as a means of intercourse. Thus, instead of their being as now between Boston and New York, for example, two or three thousand people sometimes whirled rapidly through in each direction in a single day, the only mode of intercourse was by the long journey of a solitary traveler plodding his weary way for a week or more over rough and muddy roads, on horseback or in his traveling gig. In fact, for all practical purposes, each state was in a condition of almost absolute social isolation from all the rest.

Still the extreme desirableness of some common band of union, as a means of enabling this large family of small sovereignties to maintain its standing in the world, and protect its common rights and interests, was indisputably clear, and all were agreed that something must be done. The difficulty would be in determining where and in what way the power of the small sovereignties should be curtailed in order to obtain the materials for constituting the great and general one.

General Character of the Convention

The convention met in Philadelphia, as has already been said early in May in 1787, and it continued in session all summer. Washington was elected president. At length, about the middle of September, the body concluded its labors, and agreed upon a system to be recommended to the several states for their adoption.

We are accustomed to think much of the wisdom of our ancestors, as displayed in the formation of the federal constitution, and to picture to our minds, in conceiving of the scene presented by the convention during the period of their deliberations, an assembly of calm, venerable, and patriotic men, without selfishness, without party spirit, or political animosities of any kind, but all intent only on calmly considering in friendly consultation, and harmoniously adopting, what they considered best for the interest of their common country.

But such a conception as this would be extremely visionary and unreal. The four months occupied by the debates of the body were spent in incessant controversy and conflict, nearly every man watching with great jealousy the interests of his own state, and all, or rather almost all, struggling with the greatest earnestness, and sometimes with great heat and passion, to obtain special advantages for their own special constituents. The wisdom and patriotism for which this assembly has been so renowned throughout the world in later times manifested itself in a very still small voice, which found the greatest possible difficulty in making itself heard amid the stormy conflict of selfish interest and passion with which the assembly was filled. It succeeded, however, in the end in gaining the victory, and is all the more worthy of the commendation it has received on account of the tempestuous violence of the commotion through which it led the way to a safe and happy issue at last.

Injunction of Secrecy

The proceedings of the convention were held with closed doors, and an injunction of secrecy was laid upon the members, which prohibited them from making known anything that took place. This was to save the country from the excitement and agitation which might have resulted from the publication of the debates from day to day, and the consequent arousing throughout the land of the same stormy conflict of interest and passion that raged in the convention itself. This injunction was never formally removed, but the proceedings and debates were finally published at different times and in various ways, and the subjects of controversy and causes of disagreement were made known. The principal of them were the following.

Jealousy of State Rights and State Sovereignty

One of the chief obstacles to the success of the plan of forming a united government—a difficulty which was not only great in itself but was the source and origin of a great many difficulties flowing from it—was the fact that there prevailed among all the people a great deal of love for their respective states, but very little for their common country. The whole country had scarcely yet begun to be embodied in their conceptions as a unity. It is true the various states had been bound together for many years in the pursuit of a common object, and had been, to a certain extent, united under one organization, namely, the Congress. But the great common object had now long since been accomplished, and the Congress had been considered by the people as scarcely more than a board of commissioners, acting for many independent states, and not at all as a real and genuine government for a united people.

Thus the love of country and the patriotic feeling cherished by the people had everywhere for its chief object their own particular state, and they were naturally very jealous of its independence, its sovereignty, and its rights. They were accordingly, without perhaps being particularly conscious of it, extremely reluctant to diminish the powers and prerogatives of a government which they had always loved as their own, for the benefit of a new and larger one, which, being new, they had of course not yet learned to love.

Political Conservatism

They acted under the principle of political conservatism—that is, a strong attachment to things as they are and as they have been, simply because they so are and so have been—one of the most powerful and most beneficent, and at the same time one of the blindest and most unreasonable of all the impulses of the human mind.

The tract of country through which the river Connecticut flows in the upper part of its course has long been divided into two independent states, Vermont and New Hampshire. The people on each side have grown up from infancy with strong attachments—those on the east to their native New Hampshire, and those on the west to their native Vermont. If now for any good reason of public policy it should become no matter how desirable to unite these two states into one, the people on both sides of the river would be unanimous in resisting the change, and it would require an enormous pressure of necessity, or of interest, to overcome the universal opposition to it which would be awakened.

A little farther south the same river flows through another portion of the same tract of country, the circumstances being in all respects substantially the same, except that here the territory on each side of the stream has from time immemorial formed one state instead of two. If now it should for any reason become desirable to separate these two portions and make two states—one on each side of the river—the resistance and opposition to the change would be just as invincible as in the other case. There is no reason whatever why the territory on the north should be divided by the river into two states, and on the south should form but one, except that it is so, and for several generations back it has been so—which is in fact no good reason at all; but it would very likely be actually easier to overrun and subdue by military force the whole country, than to make the river a boundary toward the south, or to abolish it as a boundary on the north. The people in one quarter would contend to the last extremity to prevent, what, under precisely similar circumstances, in respect to all the material aspects of the case, those in the other would contend with equal vehemence and persistency to retain.

This principle, though blind, and often extremely unreasonable in individual cases, is still, within proper limits, beneficent in its general operation. It often retards desirable and even necessary changes —but then perhaps it more frequently prevents useless or dangerous ones, and at any rate it gives a certain steadiness to the advance of civilization and improvement, which has a vast influence on the welfare of the human family.

Now it was the attachment of the people of the country to their respective states, and their unwillingness to curtail state prestige and power for the purpose of creating a new government in respect to which all feelings of love, respect and veneration were yet to be formed, which constituted the great difficulty in the way of organizing the proposed union.

The Question of Aristocracy and Democracy

Besides this reluctance to furnish the elements of a central power by concessions from the states, there were great differences of opinion among the statesmen assembled in respect to the proper principles on which government in general ought to rest. The most fundamental of these differences related to the question between the democratic and the aristocratic systems—that is, whether the system should be so arranged that the basis of power should rest equally upon the whole mass of the community, or should be put in the hands of the better portions of it—the term democracy importing a government by the whole people, and aristocracy by the better classes—meaning by those the more intelligent and wealthy classes. At the present day it is the almost universal opinion that the former is the true principle, and that all attempts to confine the governing power to the wise and the good, only results in conferring it upon the cunning and the bad, and creates a class that exercise their superior wisdom, if superior wisdom they have, mainly in securing and maintaining for themselves privileges and advantages, which are denied to the classes excluded. In the times immediately succeeding the revolution, however, the contrary opinion prevailed, as it does still in England. The general opinion was that in some way or other the preponderance of power ought to be retained in the hands of the higher classes, and endless were the debates on the principles and tests by which the individuals who constituted the higher classes, worthy of being the chief depositories of power, should be ascertained. Should a property qualification be the test? If so, how rich must a man be to be a voter—or to be a member of Congress—or a president? Some thought that it would be safe to elect a president who was not worth more than a thousand dollars, while others were of opinion that not less than two hundred thousand would be sufficient to make him really trustworthy.

Then, too, what *kinds* of property were to be included in making up the qualifications? Should it be real estate alone? Should slaves be reckoned as property for this end, and if so, should they also be considered as property in respect to the ratio of taxation?

On these and similar points, and on the infinite number of details involved in them, there was a vast diversity of opinion, and it seemed for a long time impossible that the convention could ever come to a common understanding in respect to them. The subject of property qualifications in politics is always an exceedingly unmanageable one.

The Union

Diversities of Opinion in Respect to Details

Besides these differences of opinion on really important principles, there were endless diversities and interminable discussions about details, many of which were of very little significance, and were scarcely to be reasoned about at all—such as of what precise number should the new senate and new house consist?—how often should they be elected, and for precisely what term should they serve?—what should be the limit of age to make men eligible?—how should the chief executive officer be chosen?—what should be his title and how long should he serve? On this latter point some argued strenuously for one year, some for two, others for three, four, five, and six—each speaker attaching great importance to his own particular view. Then how should the president be chosen—by the people, or by the state governments, or by the national senate, or by the house of representatives? The discussion of these and many other similar points of detail consumed a large portion of the time of the assembly, without appearing to lead to any satisfactory result.

Parties

In regard to the points above mentioned, the differences of opinion were those of individuals rather than of parties, as they did not involve the interests of any particular classes of states, or of any of the great industrial avocations of the country. There were certain great questions, however, on which distinct parties were formed, according as the interests of different classes of states, and of different sections of the country, were involved in them. The two great divisions of this character were those arising from the distinction of large and small states, and of the products of free and slave labor.

The Large and Small States

There was then as now a great difference among the different states, in respect not only to extent of territory, but to the wealth and population of the inhabitants. The small states were, of course, interested in framing the new government in such a way as to sustain as much as possible the equality of the states in the administration of it; while the large states would desire that the system to be adopted should assume a form to give the different districts of the country a share in the control, proportioned in some degree to the number and the wealth of the inhabitants. If the people of the whole country were blended into one community, for the management of affairs of common interest to all, then some of the small states, comprising but a limited territory and containing few inhabitants, would be lost, as it were, in the great mass, and their influence would be comparatively insignificant.

On the other hand, if the general people were not so blended, but if the distinction of states was still kept up in the general government, so as to give to all the states an equal voice, which is what the smaller states demanded, then thousands of people in one part of the country—individually as wealthy and as important as any—would have less influence in the management of public affairs than hundreds might have in another.

This was a vital question. Indeed the basis of the whole structure depended upon the disposal of it. It gave rise to earnest and almost perpetual conflicts in the convention, and once or twice came near bringing the whole undertaking to an end.

Free and Slave States

A great many exceedingly important questions arose out of the distinction of free and slave states which led to the formation of parties on this subject too. One point was the continuance of the importation of slaves. The slave states wished that the general government should have no control over this subject; the others thought that, whatever opinion might be entertained in respect to continuing to hold men already slaves in bondage, the business of making new victims, by causing them to be seized in their native land and brought across the ocean to be sold into eternal bondage in America, was barbarous and cruel, and ought no longer to be endured.

Navigation Laws

The subject of investing the proposed general government with power to enact navigation laws—by which are meant laws tending to confine the commerce of the country to ships built by the people of the country—was one on which the slave and free states took different sides. The people of the slave states did not build ships, and they had no particular facilities for building them. Their industry was confined to raising certain staple productions to be sent abroad, and they wished the privilege of exporting them, and of bringing in return cargoes of manufactured goods, by any ships that could be obtained most easily, wherever they might be built. The free states, on the other hand, were greatly interested in ship building and navigation, and they naturally thought it important to the country at large that this interest should be protected and fostered by proper legislation.

Wise Counsels Prevail in the End

In the midst of the turmoil and confusion made by the earnest and sometimes angry debates to which all these various questions gave rise there was, after all, as has already been said, a still small voice of patriotism, moderation, and wisdom, which made itself heard, and succeeded, little by little and step by step, as the debates went on, in so shaping the course and action of the body that a fair, equitable, and in almost every respect excellent system, was developed and adopted in the end. Several of the subjects of disagreement above mentioned were settled by compromise.

The Two Compromises

There were two principal compromises made. The first—in respect to the *small and large states*—was that the small states should be favored by having an equal representation with the large in the national senate, and the large ones—which were then chiefly slave states—by having three-fifths of the number of their slaves reckoned in determining the basis of representation in the lower house. The other—in respect to the interests of *free and slave labor*—was that the new government should have power to enact laws favoring northern ships and shipping, and that on the other hand the south should not be prevented from importing slaves until after the expiration of twenty years.

General Features of the System that was Adopted

The plan finally adopted by the Convention to be recommended to the states was in its essential features as follows.

1. The people of all the states were to be united and blended, in respect to the exercise of certain specified governmental functions, into one great community, the whole territory to be divided into districts containing an equal population, each one of which was to send one member as delegate to a body to be called the House of Representatives.

2. Every state as a state was to designate two persons who were to be members of another body called the Senate. These senators, however, were not to be considered as ambassadors from the states, or delegates especially representing the state governments appointing them, for they had no power to act for the state governments, or to bind them in any way; nor after their appointment were they to have any official communication with the state governments. The states designated them, but after being so designated they were each bound in their deliberations to act with a view to the interests of the whole country. They could not in fact act as in any sense depositories of the political power of the States appointing them, for as members of the general government their functions were confined entirely to a class of subjects over which the states, *as states,* were expressly to resign all jurisdiction and control.

3. The third and the great distinguishing feature of the new system, as compared with that of the old Confederation was the establishment of an executive department with the powers conferred upon it to carry into effect all the measures and enactments of the general government, by having liberty to enter everywhere upon the territory of the several states, to purchase and hold land there for

forts, arsenals, navy-yards, custom houses, and all other necessary national purposes, to establish its own courts, and appoint its own officers, and other functionaries there, and thus to execute at once by its own direct agency, its own measures, and to supply itself with all the necessary means, both of men and money, for carrying its measures into effect by its power over the individual citizen.

The head of this executive system was to be styled the president of the United States, and all the necessary machinery was provided for of custom houses, and custom house officers to collect duties, and assessors and collectors of taxes, and courts, and sheriffs, and commissioners, to execute the laws, and everything else to enable the new government to act itself, at once, by its own machinery, instead of calling upon the several states by requisitions to act for them.

Surrender of Power by the States

By accepting and ratifying the proposed constitution, the states were to surrender entirely and forever, all that portion of the power that had previously belonged to them as sovereignties, which pertained to certain subjects of general interest therein referred to the general government, in order that in respect to these subjects the people of the whole land might exercise sovereignty in respect to those subjects, as one people. These subjects were:

1. All the relations of the country with foreign nations, including the Indian tribes, whether friendly relations as those of commerce in time of peace, or hostile in time of war.
2. The coining and regulation of the national money.
3. The postal system.

The Judicial Department

The plan of the general government was made complete by the establishment of a complete system of national courts to try and decide all questions arising between different states, or individuals of different states, and to punish all offenses against the national laws. This system consisted of district courts for the various portions of the country, and a supreme court to sit as a court of appeal at the seat of government.

The Plan Submitted to the Confederate Congress

As the Confederate Congress, or the Continental Congress as it was still sometimes called, had continued to exist, and perform some feeble functions, it was deemed proper to transmit the report of the Convention to them, to be by them communicated to the several states. The Congress was at that time in session at New York. There was some debate in that body on the question whether to transmit the document to the states or not, but it was finally decided to do so, and copies of the proposed constitution were sent to the governments of all the states, with a view to calling conventions of the people to consider the question of ratifying it. This was late in September, 1787.

The Ratification

The question of the ratification of the new constitution was to be passed upon in conventions of the people chosen for the purpose, because the proposed organization was considered not as a compact between the state governments but a new general government formed by the people. Conventions were accordingly chosen in nearly all the states, and long debates and discussions ensued in each of them. It was not till three months after the proposed form was laid before the country that the first state population ratified it, and that was Delaware. The decision of the rest came in very slowly. There was great difference of opinion—both on principles and on details—which led to much disputing and great delay. As one after another of the conventions came to a decision, some voted to ratify conditionally; others ratified absolutely, but recommended modifications of the plan. It was nearly a year before the ratifications of ten states were secured. This number was thought to be sufficient to justify putting the new government into operation, and measures were accordingly adopted for that purpose. The other three states came in afterward. North Carolina and Rhode Island were the two last, and they did not come in until after the first president had been chosen.

ELECTION OF PRESIDENT

Without waiting any longer for these last doubting and hesitating parties to come to a conclusion, the people of the country prepared to put the new system into operation, leaving the doubters to join them afterward or not as they chose. The first step was the election of the president, on whom would devolve the duty of organizing the new government and setting the machinery in motion.

It seemed to be assumed as a matter of course by the whole country that Washington was the person on whom this duty would devolve. The election was, however, regularly held, according to the prescribed form, and Washington was unanimously chosen.

CHAPTER IX
INAUGURATION OF THE GOVERNMENT

Departure of Washington from Mount Vernon

Washington was officially notified of his election as the first president of the United States on the 14th of April, 1789. His preparations for departure from home were already in an advanced state of forwardness, as the certainty of the fact of his election had been known for some time—the notification being only an official formality. Two days after it was received he set out on his journey to New York, which was to be for a time the seat of the government about to be organized.

Escort of Neighbors and Friends

After bidding farewell to his family and people, Washington commenced his journey, but was met at a short distance from the boundaries of the estate by a cavalcade of gentlemen of Virginia, his neighbors and friends, who had made arrangements to assemble in the neighborhood and escort him as far as Alexandria, which was about ten miles up the river from Mount Vernon, and constituted the first stage of the journey.

This cavalcade was ready, and advanced to meet the president as he left the confines of the estate. One of the party in receiving him made a brief address, in which, after alluding to the great services which he had rendered the country, and through which he had become the object of universal respect and veneration, proceeded to speak more particularly of the benefits which he had been the means of conferring upon his neighbors and friends in the district where he resided, the useful public works which he had promoted, and the various enterprises for promoting the welfare and prosperity of the region which had been sustained and carried to a successful issue through his exertion and influence. They mourned the loss which they were to sustain by his being again about to leave them; but his country called him, they said, and they wished him to go. Finally they bade him farewell, commending him, during his absence, to the protection of heaven in the following words:

> "To that Being who maketh and unmaketh at His will we commend you, and after the accomplishment of the arduous business to which you are called, may He restore to us again the best of men and the most beloved fellow-citizen."

Washington's Reply

Washington was much moved by this manifestation of affectionate and respectful regard from the people of the country around. To their address he made the following reply:

> "Gentlemen:—Although I ought not to conceal, yet I cannot describe the painful emotions which I felt in being called upon to determine whether I would accept or refuse the presidency of the United States. The unanimity in the choice, the opinion of my friends communicated from different parts of Europe, as well as America, and an ardent desire on my own part to be instrumental in cementing the goodwill of my countrymen toward each other, have induced an acceptance. Those who know me best, and you my fellow-citizens are from your situation in that number, know better than any others, my love of retirement is so great that no earthly consideration short of a conviction of duty could have prevailed upon me to depart from my resolution never more to take any share in transactions of a public nature: for at my age, and in my circumstances, what prospects or advantages could I propose to myself from embarking again on the tempestuous and uncertain ocean of public life?
>
> "I do not feel myself under the necessity of making public declarations in order to convince you, gentlemen, of my

attachment to yourselves and regard for your interests. The whole tenor of my life has been open to your inspection, and my past actions, rather than my present declarations, must be the pledge of my future conduct.

"In the meantime, I thank you most sincerely for the expressions of kindness contained in your valedictory address. It is true, that just after having bid adieu to my domestic connections, this tender proof of your friendship is but too well calculated still further to awaken my sensibility, and increase my regret at parting from the enjoyments of private life.

"All that now remains for me is to commit myself and you to the protection of that beneficent Being, who, on a former occasion, happily brought us together after a long and distressing separation. Perhaps the same gracious Providence will again indulge me. Unutterable sensations must, then, be left to more expressive silence, while from an aching heart I bid you all, my affectionate friends and kind neighbors, farewell!"

Progress of the Journey

When the party arrived at Alexandria, Washington found the inhabitants assembled to receive him with public honors. There was also another escort formed there, ready to conduct him on the next stage of his journey, which was to Georgetown. Thus he went on with escort after escort. When he reached the Schuylkill just before entering Philadelphia, he found the bridge across that river decorated with a triumphal arch of laurel, with laurel shrubbery at each end of it. As Washington passed under the arch, a civic crown, adorned with sprigs of laurel, was let down and placed upon his head by a boy concealed from view.

On the farther side of the bridge Washington found the road lined with crowds of people, who rent the air with acclamations as he passed along. Thus advancing, conducted by the authorities of the city, and followed by his escort—he entered the town, and proceeded to Independence Hall, the edifice in which the Continental Congress had held its sessions when the Declaration of Independence was passed, and where the document was signed. In this hall a grand reception had been arranged for him, and here he was welcomed anew, with addresses and congratulations by the public authorities and their friends, and by shouts of acclamation from the vast crowds of people assembled in the streets around.

Universal Enthusiasm

The excitement and enthusiasm of the people seemed to increase as the journey went on. After leaving Philadelphia his course lay up the Delaware River. As he passed along the people everywhere gathered to see him. Every town appointed delegates of its citizens to go out to meet him as he approached. Entertainments were given in honor of him and addresses made, expressive of congratulation and joy. Military companies were called out to escort him from place to place, and at all the principal points his arrival was announced by the ringing of bells and the firing of cannon. In a word his progress through the country was marked by the applause and the rejoicings of the whole population.

Celebration at the Bridge at Trenton

One of the principal scenes of this grand ovation was enacted at Trenton, where Washington, about twelve years before, performed his grand exploit of passing his army across the Delaware in the night, in boats, among the floating ice, and in a snowstorm, and surprising and capturing a large British force in the town, thus gaining one of the most important victories of the war. This was accordingly thought to be a fitting place for some special celebration.

The arrangements were made, and the ceremonies were conducted by the ladies of Trenton. They caused a triumphal arch to be erected upon a bridge across a small stream near the town, which had been the scene of some of the most important operations connected with the battle, and adorned it with wreaths of laurel and with a profusion of flowers—some gathered from the fields and forests and some from the gardens and conservatories in the town.

Upon the crown of the arch was an inscription formed ingeniously of evergreen leaves and flowers, and containing the words:

December 26th, 1776.

This was the date of the battle. On the sweep of the arch below were the words, also formed of leaves and flowers:

The Defender of the Mothers will be the Protector of the Daughters.

Washington was received at this arch, and welcomed on his passage through it, by a large procession of the ladies of Trenton. They arranged themselves, as he approached, on each side of the road, the children on one side dressed in white, and each bearing a basket of flowers, and the young ladies upon the other, dressed in the same manner; while the mothers stood in a row on each side behind.

After Washington had passed through the arch he stopped to listen to a song of welcome, in two stanzas, which was to be sung by a choir of singers stationed near. These stanzas were written for the occasion, and the idea which they conveyed was that of the striking contrast between the circumstances of his crossing the river in the face of desperate and implacable enemies twelve years before, and those which marked his transition now, welcomed by the grateful and joyful acclamations of friends, who owed to him their own personal protection and the salvation of their country. The words were as follows:

> Welcome, mighty chief; once more!
> Welcome to this grateful shore!
> *Now* no mercenary foe
> Aims again the fatal blow—
>   Aims at thee the fatal blow.
>
> Virgins fair and matrons grave,
> Whom thy conquering arm did save,
> Build for thee triumphal bowers.
> Strew, ye fair, his way with flowers!
>   Strew your hero's way with flowers!

Inauguration of the Government

Washington, president elect.

As these last words were sung the children strewed the road with flowers from their baskets, and Washington and his suite passed on into the town—the incessant ringing of bells and booming of guns adding excitement to the scene.

Arrival at New York

In due time Washington arrived at his place of destination, New York, where, on account of circumstances which cannot he here particularly detailed, it had been decided that the new government should be organized and set in operation.

Entrance into New York

The land journey of the party ended at Elizabethtown, where at Elizabethtown Point, on the Passaic River, an elegant barge had been provided to convey the president and his suite to the city. He had requested that his entrance to the city might be made in a private manner and without parade; but the people would not consent to this, and arrangements had accordingly been made for an imposing aquatic procession to conduct the party from the place of embarkation at Elizabethtown Point along the channel between Staten Island and the mainland, and thence up the harbor to the city.

The Barges

The barge in which Washington himself was to be conveyed was constructed expressly for the occasion. It was manned by thirteen chief pilots, masters of pilot vessels belonging to the harbor. They were dressed in white, and were commanded by a naval officer of high rank. This barge was attended and followed by other barges, all gaily decorated with flags and banners. These vessels conveyed the heads of the departments who had held office under the confederation, and who had not yet been replaced, and other official personages of high rank, together with several distinguished citizens of New York who had been honored with invitations to join in the procession. They advanced in regular order, and as they proceeded along the shores of Staten Island and turned to go up the harbor they were met by great numbers of other boats coming from town, all likewise gaily decorated. The boats, as they met the approaching procession, turned aside and waited on their oars for the barges to pass, and then fell into the rear, thus forming, as the fleet advanced toward the city, a long and imposing procession.

One of the boats which closely accompanied the President's barge, contained an instrumental band playing marches, military airs, and other exciting music on the way; and when the head of the column drew near the landing place it passed by two vessels containing a party of ladies and gentlemen, who sang congratulatory odes as Washington's barge approached.

The various vessels lying at anchor in the harbor were all decorated with flags, and the ships of war of different nations that chanced to be present at the time, manned their yards, and saluted the passing procession by the lowering of their colors, the huzzas of the seamen, and the thundering of the guns.

THE LANDING

Preparations for the landing had been made at Murray's wharf, at the foot of Murray Street. The wharf itself and all the streets adjoining it, were thronged with spectators who rent the air with their acclamations, the sounds of which were mingled with the ringing of bells from all the steeples, and the booming of guns. On landing from the barge, Washington was received by Governor Clinton, the governor of New York; General Knox, one of his former companions in arms; and many other officers, both civil and military, and other persons of distinction. A carriage had also been provided for him to convey him through the streets, with a carpet laid down for him to walk upon, in order to reach it. An officer advanced also, with the military salute, and announced himself as the commander of the life-guard which had been provided to escort the president to the governor's house, and asked for his excellency's orders.

Washington was embarrassed rather than gratified by these marks of homage, such as in Europe would be accorded to a sovereign prince at a coronation. He replied to the officer of the guard that he might proceed with his duty according to the arrangements which had been made by the committee, and he declined the carriage, saying it would be more agreeable to him to walk.

The Procession to the Governor's

The guard, together with the various officers and persons of distinction who had come to accompany Washington to his lodgings, formed a long military and civic procession, under the escort of which the president at once proceeded through the streets toward the house of the governor. The streets were so thronged that it was with difficulty that the procession could make its way. Arches had been erected here and there, and every house was decorated with flags, banners, garlands of flowers, and inscriptions of congratulation and welcome.

The president proceeded in this manner to the house of the governor, where he was to be entertained. He met at the dinner table a number of civil and military officers and other persons of distinction, and in the evening the city was given up to illuminations and fireworks, and to other demonstrations of festivity and joy.

The Inauguration

The formal induction of the president into office, took place on the 30th of April, about a week after his arrival in the city. The ceremony was performed at Federal Hall, so called, a public edifice which stood in Wall Street, on the site of the present custom house. There was a wide balcony upon the front of the building which extended over the sidewalk, and afforded a fine position for administering the oath in view of an immense concourse of spectators that assembled in the street below, and at the windows and upon the roofs of the surrounding buildings. There was a roof over the balcony, with tall columns supporting it, leaving the balcony itself, which was quite large, almost entirely open above the balustrade to public view.

In the center of the balcony had been placed a table covered with a crimson cloth, and upon the table a magnificently bound Bible, intended to be used for administering the oath, reposed upon a crimson velvet cushion. One or two armchairs were placed near the table.

As soon as Washington and those accompanying him who were to take part in the ceremony appeared upon the balcony, they were received by long and loud acclamations from the immense throng that had assembled. Washington was attired in the court dress of those times, with knee buckles, and long silk stockings, shoes with silver clasps, a sword, and powdered hair dressed with a silken bag behind.

Administration of the Oath

After advancing to the front of the balcony to receive and acknowledge the congratulations of the people, Washington stepped back and took his seat in one of the chairs near the table until silence should be restored. When all was still he arose again and advanced to the front of the balcony; accompanied by John Adams, the vice-president elect, on one side, and by Robert R. Livingston, the chancellor of the state of New York, who was to administer the oath, on the other. Several other gentlemen of distinction stood in the rear, among whom were Roger Sherman, Alexander Hamilton, General Knox, Baron Steuben, and others.

The secretary of state, Mr. Otis, raised the Bible from the table on its velvet cushion, and held it in a convenient position for the performance of the ceremony. The chancellor then read the oath, enunciating the words in a very slow, distinct and audible manner, while the vast throngs in the streets, and at the windows, on the roofs and in the balconies of the houses around, listened in solemn silence.

Washington uttered his response in the same distinct and emphatic manner, and then reverently kissed the book which the secretary held before him for that purpose.

Rejoicings

As soon as this ceremony was concluded the chancellor came forward to the front of the balcony, and waving his hand to the vast audience, he called out with a loud voice,

"Long live George Washington, President of the United States!"

This announcement that the ceremony of taking the oath was completed, was received with one loud and universal burst of acclamation from the assembled multitude. At the same moment a flag was run up the staff upon the cupola of the building, as a signal to the men stationed at the guns on the battery, and the air was instantly filled with the roar of artillery, and with the ringing of the bells of every steeple and tower in the city.

Concluding Ceremonies

Washington then, after bowing once more to the assembled multitude, retired from the balcony, and proceeding to the principal legislative hall within the building, he delivered his inaugural address, in the hearing of a large audience, consisting of the members of Congress and other persons of distinction. On the conclusion of the address, the whole legislative body, with the executive officers of the government and many invited guests, proceeded in order to St. Paul's church, where the ceremonies of the day were closed by appropriate religious services.

Influential Men Associated with Washington in the Government

Among the most prominent men who were politically associated with Washington in the early administration of public affairs, and whose influence was most decided in first shaping the institutions and directing the policy of the government, perhaps the most conspicuous were John Adams, Alexander Hamilton, Thomas Jefferson, and James Madison. These persons had all taken a very active and prominent part in forming the federal constitution, and also, by their commanding influence among the people of the country, in promoting the ratification of it by the states; and they were now severally appointed by the president, or had been elected by the people, to occupy prominent positions in the organization and administration of the new government.

John Adams

John Adams was the vice president, and by virtue of this office, the president of the senate. He was a citizen of Boston, and the leading representative of the New England States in the counsels of the general government. He had occupied this position in fact during the whole period of the revolutionary war, having been from the beginning a very prominent and leading member of the Continental Congress. Someone, on examining the records of the proceedings of that body, found that Adams had been a member of ninety committees, and chairman of twenty-five of them. On all the questions that arose during the whole period previous to the commencement of the presidency of Washington—including the conduct of the war, the management of negotiations with foreign powers at the conclusion of it, and the forming of the federal constitution, his agency was very active, and was of the most important character. He was appointed as one of the commissioners to the court of Versailles to negotiate the treaty of peace, and during his residence abroad he acquired a distinguished reputation among the European courts, where his influence in promoting the interests of the American government was of the most marked and striking character.

He was now between fifty and sixty years of age, and his ripe experience, his intimate knowledge of public affairs, the weight and dignity of his character, his great ascendancy over the minds of his countrymen, especially of the people of New England, and his exalted position as president of the senate, combined to render him a very safe and able counselor, and Washington relied greatly upon his judgment in the decision of every important question.

Alexander Hamilton

Hamilton was about twenty years younger than Adams, being at the time of the inauguration of President Washington about thirty-two years of age. Young as he was, however, he was already greatly distinguished. He entered the army of the revolution from Columbia College, New York, when he was about nineteen years of age, and there soon attracted the attention of General Washington, who appointed him one of his aids, and he remained attached personally to the general during the whole period of the war.

At the close of the war he studied law and was admitted to the bar. He immediately began to acquire an eminent position, but was soon diverted from his profession by being elected a member of Congress under the old confederation, and from that time he devoted himself entirely to political life. He very soon acquired great distinction in Congress, and he took a very active part in the formation of the federal constitution, and subsequently exerted a great influence in securing the adoption of it through the efforts which he made to explain the principles of the system to the people at large, and the eloquence and ability with which he advocated them

The Federalist

The chief vehicle through which Hamilton and those acting with him conveyed their explanations and reasoning, in respect to the federal constitution, to the public was a series of periodical essays which they published under the name of the Federalist. Hamilton was himself the principal writer of the articles of this work, though he was greatly aided by Madison and by some other powerful coadjutors. The Federalist exerted great influence at the time in clearly explaining to the people of the country the principles of the new constitution, and in securing its adoption; and the work has since assumed the character of a standard authority of the highest value, as an authentic contemporaneous exposition of the views and intentions of the founders of the constitution, and of the proper interpretation to be put upon the language of the document in all cases of doubt or disagreement that may arise in the practical working of the system.

Hamilton's Public Career

Hamilton was appointed by the president to the office of secretary of the treasury; for, in addition to the other evidences of superior statesmanship which his writings had evinced, he had shown himself extremely well informed on questions of finance. Washington, in addition to the confidence which he had in his ability as a statesman, felt a strong personal affection for him as a man. This affection had grown up in the course of the years of danger, anxiety, and suffering which they had spent together during the war. He consequently regarded him not only as an able coadjutor in his government, but also as a dear and highly valued personal friend.

Hamilton managed the affairs of his department with great ability while he remained in office. He was subsequently called to render public services of the highest importance in various capacities, both civil and military, and finally became in the minds of his countrymen an object of universal and very exalted estimation.

His Untimely End

At length, when he was nearly fifty years of age, he became involved in some difficulty with Aaron Burr, arising from a rude demand made upon him by Burr to explain or apologize for something which he had said in his political writings. Hamilton refused to do either, and Burr challenged him to a duel.

The duel was fought at Hoboken, near New York, with much formality and ceremony, and Hamilton was slain. The excitement of the public mind awakened by this duel, and the shock universally produced by the fatal termination of it, moved the people of this country more deeply than any other event of the kind that has ever occurred.

The Fundamental Question of Politics

Although the leading statesmen of the country had finally agreed to support the frame of government established by the federal constitution, it was, after all, only by the spirit of compromise and of mutual concession that they did so; for, as has already been shown in a previous chapter, there was a serious difference of opinion among them in respect to the fundamental principles on which government, in modern civilized societies, ought to be founded. The question which separated them was the one which divides public opinion at the present day in all enlightened nations, and constitutes the most general and most important line of demarcation between the great political parties that are contending against each other in every free community. The question is this:

Ought governmental institutions to be so framed as to retain political power as much as possible in the hands of the wise and the good, or so as to diffuse it equally throughout the whole community, and thus to give every man that is subject to it a just and equal share?

In all the governments of Europe the former has always been the principle acted upon—the wise and good being understood to mean practically the rich and powerful. The struggle, however, between the two sets of opinions has been going on there very vigorously for many years—one party, calling themselves conservatives, making every effort to retain political power and influence in the hands of the smallest possible number—and they of the upper classes—on the theory that they are more trustworthy and better informed than the mass of the community, and may accordingly be taken for the wise and the good; and the other endeavoring to diffuse and extend the elements of power, so as to admit larger and larger portions of the population to the exercise of their proper portion of it.

Opinions of Adams and Hamilton

This same division of political opinions existed in America, though in a somewhat mitigated form; one class being inclined to bring the mass of the people much more fully, completely, and directly into the possession of political power than the other. Adams and Hamilton were representatives and leaders of the first class, Jefferson and Madison of the second.

It is true that Adams and Hamilton, and the men with whom they acted, were by no means in favor of a legal and formal exclusion of the humbler classes from all participation in government, as in England; but while they were willing to give all a vote in the first instance, and thus to make the government a popular one in theory, still they were inclined to favor such arrangements, in regulating the actual working of the machine, as should practically keep the control in the hands of the few.

A Monarchy Impossible

Indeed Hamilton, it is said, would have been inclined to favor a monarchy as the best form of government for America, if a monarchy had been possible. But he knew well that this was out of the question, for the reason that it is impossible to improvise a king. It takes many centuries to make a king. It is true that a conqueror may place one of his generals, or a congress of sovereigns some younger son of a royal family, in a gilded chair on a dais, in the capital of some subjugated country, and call him a king; but he is not really a king, nor can they possibly make him one. He is a chief magistrate created by appointment or election, holding his office only for a brief term, and liable to be suddenly ejected from it at any time for real or supposed misbehavior.

The brothers and son of the first Napoleon were such kings as these. So were, or are, Louis Phillippe, Otho and George of Greece, and Leopold of Belgium; and we may one of these days have such a king made for Canada. But in forming our national constitution even those who were inclined to favor monarchical institutions as the best, provided there existed in the state a royal family which had been spreading its roots in the history and heart of the nation for so many centuries that no trace or tradition remained of the origin of its power, knew perfectly well that where no such dynasty existed it would be impossible to supply its place by any artificial process of appointment or election.

Opinions of Jefferson and Madison

Jefferson and Madison on the other hand were utterly opposed to aristocratic or monarchical systems of government on principle. They were the leaders and representatives of a class of statesmen, whose policy was to lay the foundations of government on a very broad basis—as broad as humanity itself. They considered this the most just and at the same time the safest system, and the best for all concerned. They wished to carry down the foundations of political power until it should come to a bearing, and find a support, in the regularly expressed will of every man who was to be subject to its jurisdiction, and to bring the action of the government as directly, as closely, and as invariably as possible under the control of the general popular voice. They thought it the best policy to give up all hope of making the government better than the majority of the people—to allow the popular determination—as ascertained by a fair and formal expression of the will of all classes of the community—to be carried into effect, whether right or wrong in the opinion of individuals—and if evils should exist, to aim at rectifying them by changing the national will, and not thwarting it or controlling it by any higher authority constituted for this purpose.

Equal Political Rights for All Men the Only Safe Policy of Government

The principle of giving every man a voice in the ultimate control and management of public affairs, constitutes altogether the most stable and secure foundation for government, for under such a system every man, knowing that he has his fair share of influence in determining the course of public policy, feels a personal interest in the government, and a wish that it should be sustained; whereas, under the other system there is always a large class of men, who, having no voice in the government, must be held in subjection by it. This requires the organization and maintenance of a large and permanent military force, and even then the country which holds a large portion of the population in this condition is continually exposed to the outbreak of riots, insurrections and revolutions.

For the first fifty years of the existence of this government, during which universal suffrage as the foundation of government, and a control, as direct, immediate, and complete as possible, over all the measures of the government by the will of the whole people, prevailed, not one tenth part of the military force, in proportion to the population, was required to maintain the authority of the government, that has been deemed necessary in France and England, and in all other monarchical countries during the same period.

And when at last our great rebellion came, it had its origin solely in causes arising from the fact that in a large section of the country nearly half the population were deprived of all personal and political rights; so that our own terrible troubles, when they finally came, arose solely from our refusal to carry out fully the principles of the system.

The Only Just as Well as the Only Safe Policy

Jefferson considered the system of equal rights for all men as not only the safest, but as the only just system. A man born in any country had naturally an equal right with all the rest to a voice in determining the policy on which his life and his welfare, and those of his wife and children depended. For one portion of the community to exclude the rest from all share in the control, on the ground that they themselves were the best judges of the proper measures to be adopted to promote the general welfare, seemed to him to be the perpetration of a great injustice and wrong.

The friends of equal rights in those days did not consider ignorance and poverty as constituting a just ground for depriving a man of his voice in the management of public affairs. There are very few men in any community who are competent to form an enlightened opinion in respect to the details of legislation—that is, there are in any community very few statesmen. But a man in exercising the right of suffrage does not assume to judge of the details of measures for promoting the public good, but only to decide to what man or party of men he will prefer to commit the keeping of his interests and those of his class, in the determination of those measures. And he has a right to that privilege.

The Right of Suffrage the Safeguard of the Poor

Indeed the poorer, more ignorant, and more miserable a man is, the more indispensable to him is his vote. It is his protection. It may constitute almost his chief claim to the consideration of those around him. A man of wealth and high standing has so many other modes of exerting an influence on public opinion, and on the policy and measures of government, that his mere vote is of comparatively little consequence to him. Deprive a millionaire of his vote and you diminish his political influence in an almost inappreciable degree. But a poor man's vote is politically his all. If he and those situated as he is are deprived of it, they lose all the means of protection they have against the enactment of laws pressing heavily upon them, and tending to fix and perpetuate their degradation and poverty.

Position of Jefferson in Washington's Government

Jefferson was appointed by Washington to the office of secretary of state under the new government. Although still young he had occupied a very prominent position before the public for many years. He was a Virginian, and bad exerted a great influence in shaping the institutions and policy of his state. He was a member of the Continental Congress and took a very prominent part in the deliberations of that body. It was by him that the first draft of the Declaration of Independence was made.

Some time after the close of the war he was sent to France as United States Minister at the French court, and it was from this position that he was called by Washington to a seat in his cabinet as secretary of state. In this office he had charge of all the foreign relations of the government, and all its intercourse with European powers.

During his whole political career Jefferson was uniform and consistent in his efforts so to shape the fundamental institutions, both of his state and of the nation, as to secure to every man an equal voice in the general direction of public affairs, and equal rights in every respect before the law. He did all in his power to promote the abolition of slavery in Virginia—and finding this impracticable, he was the means of securing the adoption of effectual measures for preventing the extension of the system into the unsettled territories then within the national jurisdiction. If the policy which he so earnestly recommended had been fully adopted by his countrymen, the nation would have been saved the sacrifice of a million of lives, and of five thousand million dollars in property, which the consent that it gave to the depriving of a large fraction of the population of all personal and civil rights, was destined in the end to cost it.

James Madison

Madison was not one of Washington's cabinet officers. He was a member of the House of Representatives, and his ability as a speaker, conjoined with the great reputation which he had acquired throughout the country by the prominent part which he had taken in framing the federal constitution, and in promoting the adoption of it by the states, and by the people, soon gave him a commanding influence in that body. Washington too, felt a great confidence in his political judgment and experience, and often consulted him on the proper course to be pursued in the various important emergencies occurring. His name has thus become associated with those of Adams, Hamilton, Jefferson, and others, as among the leading men under whose guidance and direction the first movements of the vast system of government established by the constitution of the United States were made.

Incipient Divergency of Political Opinion

It has already been said that Adams and Hamilton, and a large class of politicians sympathizing with them, were inclined to favor what is called a strong government, that is, one in which the political institutions and usages should be so framed as to keep the control as much as possible in the hands of the more respectable, more wealthy, and better educated classes of society, thus producing a concentrated and in some respects an insulated authority, while Jefferson and Madison, representing another class, were more inclined to diffuse and distribute the elements of power, in order to give it the widest possible basis, and to bring as directly as possible within the reach of every man his fair portion of control over the measures and the policy, which, affecting the general welfare, were of common interest to all. These diversities of opinion, though they existed from the beginning, did not immediately manifest themselves decidedly in such a way as to produce divided councils; though a divergence soon commenced which rapidly widened and extended, until the foundation was laid for the organization of two great parties, between which a continued struggle was carried on with great earnestness and vigor for many years.

The First Test Question

The first occasion on which these different theories of government were brought to bear upon a practical question was, as it would seem, not a very serious one. It related only to the forms and ceremonies, and points of etiquette, which should be observed by the new government, and especially by the president, in his official intercourse with Congress and with the people, and also with the representatives of foreign powers. The president was aware that there was a certain importance to be attached to the beginning that he should make in these respects, inasmuch as the practices which he should observe would be very likely to become precedents for succeeding administrations.

He accordingly addressed formal inquiries to several of the leading men around him, requesting their views on these points.

The answers to these queries revealed quite an important difference of opinion among the statesmen consulted, in respect to the proper system of forms and usages to be observed in the administration of a republican government. Those who, in their general views, were inclined to favor a strong government and a restricted basis of power, were disposed to recommend more formality and ceremony and parade than those who were more democratic in their views thought desirable.

Adams's Opinion

John Adams, who, besides being influenced by the general tendency of his political opinions, had spent some years in European courts, and had become accustomed to the regal pomp and splendor usually displayed in monarchical countries, was in favor of adopting something of the same state and parade in America. His opinion was that the office of president of the United States was superior in dignity and power to any political position in the world except that of some of the European kings, and that the state and ceremony with which the functions of the office were performed ought to correspond in some degree with its exalted character.

Accordingly, Mr. Adams recommended quite an imposing system of formalities for the regulation of the president's intercourse with those about him—such as regular applications for audience through the minister of state; stated times for receiving visits; a corps of military aides, and masters of ceremonies for the presidential mansion, to guard the approaches to the audience room; regular levees to be held at appointed times in great state; formal and ceremonious entertainments, to which official persons should be invited in rotation on a regular system; and an imposing equipage for the president when appearing in public, with four or six horses, and servants and outriders in livery.

HAMILTON

Hamilton, although in his general views of government belonging to the same school with Adams, was much less advanced than he in his ideas of official ceremonial. This was owing, doubtless, to the fact that, while Adams had been for several years preceding living in the midst of the pomp and splendor of European courts, Hamilton had remained in this country, where he had held daily intercourse with the people, and understood better the democratic tendency of the age. In his reply to the president's inquiry, he took care to say that, while he considered it important for the public good that the dignity of the presidential office should be properly supported, it was still highly desirable to avoid taking so high a tone as to shock the prevalent notions of equality.

JEFFERSON

Jefferson, on the other hand, attached very little importance to these artificial modes of adding dignity to power. Adams, he thought, "had been so dazzled with the glare of nobility and royalty during his mission to England, as to be made to believe that their fascination was a necessary ingredient in government." He and those who thought with him, favored a plain republican simplicity in the action of the government, and his views in this respect as well as in others, gradually gained the ascendancy, until at length the universal sentiment of the American people has become entirely averse to all attempts to add to the prestige of office and power, by any external paraphernalia whatever.

Gradual Formation of the Great Federal and Democratic Parties

This diversity of views among the people of the country in respect to the fundamental principles of public polity, which first manifested itself, after the organization of the government, on this comparatively unimportant question of etiquette and ceremonial parade, became gradually more and more marked, until, as has already been said, it resulted in the formation of two grand parties, which struggled against each other for national ascendancy for more than half a century.

The formation of these parties was hastened, and the vigor of their animosity against each other was greatly increased, by circumstances which grew out of the French revolution, and the wars between France and England which ensued. The French revolution was the result of a struggle for equal rights for all men, against hereditary privilege and power; while England, in contending against the French republic, took the attitude of a champion of the conservative principle, so-called, that is, a reliance for the preservation of law and order in any community, on retaining the governmental control in the hands of the upper classes of society.

Of course in the contests between England and France which immediately arose, it was natural that Adams and Hamilton, and those who acted with them should sympathize with the British, while the party of Jefferson and Madison would incline to wish success to the French. In the complications which ensued, various incidents and events occurred, which, though it does not come within the limits of this series to relate them in detail—tended strongly to involve the American government in the quarrel, and of course this state of things rapidly increased the sharpness of the line which divided the two great parties, and greatly aggravated the antagonism between them.

The difficulties and embarrassments, and the harassing anxieties and cares which Washington encountered in guiding the ship of state through this stormy sea were indescribably great. He was himself often nearly overwhelmed. But his wisdom and moderation, his calmness, his justice, his caution, his inexhaustible patience and perseverance, the weight of his personal character, and the almost unbounded influence which he exerted over the minds of his countrymen, through the love and veneration with which he was universally regarded, enabled him to come out triumphant in the end.

CHAPTER X
WORKING OF THE SYSTEM

Soon Put to the Test

Immediately after the organization of the new government, and before the machinery of the system had begun to acquire the momentum and steadiness necessary to enable any machinery successfully to meet and overcome the difficulties of its work, a series of remarkable events began to occur, relating not only to the internal condition of the country, but involving also, as was intimated in the last chapter, the relations of the American government to those of foreign nations. These difficulties had the effect of bringing the new institutions somewhat prematurely to the test. To relate the course of the events which followed, and to show in what manner the system worked under this trial, would take us beyond the limits assigned to this series, which is intended to close with the establishment of the federal constitution. This concluding chapter will, accordingly, contain some additional explanations in respect to the true nature of the compound government which had been established, as it developed itself in operation, with a view of communicating to the reader a more clear conception of the essential principles and characteristics of the system.

The Anglo-Saxon Principle of Government

The principle which forms the foundation of human government, according to the ideas of the Anglo-Saxon race, seems to be this:

Any region of the earth's surface, the parts of which are so situated in relation to each other and to other regions surrounding it as to make the interests of the people inhabiting it essentially common, constitutes naturally a country; and the people of the whole region, by the act of a majority fairly ascertained, have a natural right to

Working of the System

House of Representatives in session.

establish and maintain institutions of government for the whole, the dissent of a minority notwithstanding—whether that minority is diffused throughout the whole territory or occupies exclusively some minor portion of it.

This Principle Acknowledged and Acted upon by the English People

It is true that the British government is founded, in theory—or, rather, in the verbal expression of the theory—on the sovereignty of the crown. But this is only a formality of language, retained out of respect for its antiquity. The controlling power both in determining the political institutions of the country and in administering the government is now, and has been for several centuries, the *will of the British people*.

It is, indeed, customary still to speak of the king or the queen as the sovereign, and the people as subjects; and a species of formal and ceremonious homage is customarily rendered to the crown, but this is all entirely unreal. If a king attempts to govern the country in a manner contrary to the will of the people, they resist; and if he persists, they dethrone or behead him.

The sovereignty which nominally vests in the royal family in England at the present day is a matter of poetical sentiment or state parade alone. The real supremacy is in the national will.

Different Modes of Ascertaining the National Will

Thus the real foundation of government is in England and America the same, though there are great differences in the structures built upon it. One of the most important of these is the difference in the mode of ascertaining the national will in the two countries. In England, to ascertain the preponderance of public sentiment, the attempt is made to weigh the people. In America we are content to count them.

The Consent of the Governed

The doctrine that all governments derive their just powers from the consent of the governed is to be interpreted in conformity with the fundamental principles stated above that is, by the consent of the governed—must be understood to mean the consent of a majority of all those included within the limits of a region, which, whether more or less extensive, is so situated in regard to its geographical or other conditions as that the interests of the inhabitants are essentially common. In some cases, as for example that of Switzerland or Denmark, the region may be small; in others, as in that of France, large. In either case, the right of the people to combine, and by means of a majority of voices, fairly obtained, to ordain and maintain a government over the whole, notwithstanding the dissent of any separate portion, is complete, within the limits of the region so situated.

In other words the geographical or other conditions which determine for any region of the earth's surface, a community of interests for those inhabiting it, gives to a majority of the people so inhabiting, the right to give or withhold consent in the name of all, to any government established over them.

Examples in Point

The truth of this doctrine, as a doctrine, is universally admitted and practically acted upon in England as well as in America. If, for example, the inhabitants of the Isle of Wight were to wish to establish a separate government, the answer to their claim would be that the British Islands form a group so connected together that the interests of the whole are involved in and dependent upon the condition of every part; and that the people of every part must therefore, whatever their individual preferences may be, submit to be merged in the general population of the whole; and after being allowed their fair share of influence with the rest, must consent to come under such a system of civil polity as a majority of the whole number shall decide upon.

The same is true in respect to Ireland. That island bears such a relation to the others of the group that a foreign or an independent government ruling over it would endanger the security and welfare of the whole. Ireland therefore must be content, so Englishmen maintain, to make common cause with the other islands, and to yield submission to such a government as a majority of the whole population of the islands sees fit to maintain.

THE GENERAL GOVERNMENT OF THE UNITED STATES

The general government of the United States in all the three forms which it successively assumed, had its origin in precisely this principle—not stated perhaps at the time very formally, as a matter of theory, but felt practically as a matter of fact, namely, that such were the geographical and physical features of the region occupied by these states, that the external interests so to speak, of the whole people, that is, the interests arising from their relations to the other nations of the world, were inseparably united; that no portion of this territory could be independent of the rest without endangering the rest, and that consequently it was right for the people of the whole region to unite and establish, so far as these external relations and other subjects of common interest were concerned, one common government, to include the whole within its jurisdiction.

THE GENERAL AND THE LOCAL INTERESTS REQUIRING A DIFFERENT PROVISION

There was, however, one peculiarity in the condition of the American states, which had perhaps never existed before in so marked a degree, in any political community; and that was that while in respect to their dealings with foreign nations and with the outer world at large, and to certain other functions of government more or less related to these, the interests of the whole region were common—still, on account of the great extent of the country, the diversity of soil, climate, and productions in the different portions of it, and the varying circumstances under which the original settlements were made, the *local and internal* interests of each state, as well as the ideas of the people inhabiting them, were extremely diverse. Out of this state of things, which had perhaps never existed before in so great a degree in any political community—that is, so great a unity of interest throughout the whole in respect to dealings with the world at large, conjoined with so great a diversity of ideas and interests in respect to social institutions and local legislation, in the different parts, arose the idea—which is the great fundamental principle of the American system, of dividing the jurisdiction, and organizing over the whole one government, to hold a control entire, absolute, and supreme, over certain prescribed subjects of common interest, and over each part another government, with a control equally entire, absolute, and supreme, over all the private relations of life, including social institutions and industrial pursuits of every kind.

Fundamental Idea of the General Government

It was as if the people of the whole country had assembled together as one vast community, and, after having solemnly arranged the system of the Federal Constitution, constituted the Congress, and elected Washington as the supreme executive, had addressed the new government thus:

> "We, the people of the United States, acting together for this purpose, commit to your hands the exercise of supreme governmental power, in our name, over all that portion of the public interests that we hold in common; namely, all that relates to our dealings with foreign countries, whether those of friendly communication and commerce in time of peace, or of hostilities in time of war, and with the tribes of Indians remaining within our territory, and also all that directly concerns the intercourse of the several states with each other—and these things only.
>
> "We give you full power in respect to these subjects, to adopt, through Congress, such measures as you deem necessary, and through the president and the other executive officers associated with him, to carry your measures into effect. To this end you are authorized to enter the territory of any state, whenever you may find it necessary to do so,

in order to establish custom-houses, build forts, construct arsenals, armories, navy-yards, mints, and post-offices, and post-roads—and also to appoint all necessary officers, and employ all necessary labor, for the proper discharge of the duties assigned you.

"In order to supply yourselves with funds for these purposes, you are authorized to levy duties on imports of merchandise—making them uniform throughout the country—and to collect the duties so levied on the arrival of the merchandise in the various ports, in such a manner as you may deem expedient; and to assess other taxes, if necessary.

"No state government will interfere with you or molest you in any way while engaged in the performance of these duties, but all will leave your way unobstructed and free. You, on the other hand, must confine yourselves most strictly to the special work committed to you. All the internal affairs of government, everything that relates to the social and civil institutions of society, and to the intercourse between man and man in the ordinary relations of life—everything in fact except the specific branches of public business formally assigned to you is reserved by the states for their own regulation and control. In all these things the power of the states is absolute and supreme. We enjoin it upon you most strongly, to confine your action scrupulously and strictly to your own department of duty, and not to encroach in any way, by direct or indirect means, on the jurisdiction which we reserve to ourselves in the capacity of separate populations of separate states, to exercise through state governments which we shall maintain in the several states for this purpose.

"To guard against the danger that you may thus encroach upon the proper jurisdiction of the states, or that some state may, inadvertently or otherwise, encroach upon yours, we have provided for the establishment of a solemn tribunal, to be constituted of judges who shall be men of venerable age, of ripe experience, of the highest attainments in civil and constitutional law, and of national reputation for uprightness, integrity, and knowledge of public affairs. In case you, or any state government shall pass any act, or adopt any measure which shall be deemed an encroachment on the jurisdiction of the other, the question shall be brought before this tribunal, which, after a full hearing of both sides, shall decide it; and their decision shall be conclusive and final. Whichever government, whether state or national, shall he found by this tribunal to be wrong, it shall at once yield to the decision, and retire within the limits which the decision assigns to it."

Such, expressed in the form of instructions from the people of the United States to the new government, were the powers committed to this government, and it was the work of carrying out this system that Washington, on his inauguration as president of the United States, found before him.

QUESTION OF THE SEAT OF GOVERNMENT

During the jurisdiction of the Continental Congress and the Congress of the Confederation, the seat of government, if government it might be called, was sometimes in Philadelphia, sometimes in New York, and sometimes in other places, as the exigencies of the war and the approach of danger to this place or that might require. The necessary accommodations for the few and feeble functions which those bodies possessed could be found in almost any place. But now that a real national power had been organized, which would go on increasing in the magnitude of its operations for centuries, as the wealth and population increased, it was manifest that a suitable and permanent seat of government would he required, where edifices for the accommodation of Congress, of the president, of the various departments of the government, and for the residences of foreign ministers; might be constructed, on a scale and in a style corresponding in some degree to the magnitude and extent which the business of the government might be expected in time to assume. After mature deliberation; and a full consideration of the claims of the principal existing towns to the honor of being made the seat of government, it was finally decided to found a new city for this purpose; and a site was selected by Washington himself on the banks of the Potomac, not many miles above his own estate at Mount Vernon.

The City of Washington

The place chosen was central in reference to the territory occupied by the states, and the situation was charming. By the unanimous desire of the people of the country the new capital was named Washington. The site on which it was to be built was at the confluence of two rivers, the Potomac and the Anacostia, the waters of which furnished access for vessels of great burden from the sea. It lay within the limits of the state of Maryland, but the jurisdiction over it was at once ceded to the General Government, and the city was immediately laid out, on a very extensive scale, and the construction of the necessary buildings immediately commenced.

Transfer of the Government to Washington

So much time, however, was necessarily occupied by the deliberations and discussions, the legal formalities, the drawing and examination of plans, and the works of construction, that it was not until the year 1800 that the seat of government could be transferred to the new capitol. The functions of the government have since that time centered there, and are performed on a scale of magnitude and extent comporting with the dignity and character of the Union. The appearance of the house of representatives at the present day, when assembled for the transaction of business, in the exercise of absolute power over all the foreign affairs of the country, and substantially over all the internal affairs which are of common interest, presents a very different spectacle from that of the old Confederate Congress, consisting of thirty or forty members only, and they so dilatory in their duty that it was often impossible to obtain a quorum.*[1]

In due time other national establishments were created in various parts of the country by the general government—all, however, for purposes confined strictly to the departments of business with which that government had been entrusted—namely, for the collection of

---

[1] See engraving on p. 157.

duties on imports, for the accommodation of the system of courts taking cognizance of questions of national character, for the postal system, for the management of Indian affairs, and for the naval and military defense of the country. There were navy yards established at Pensacola, at Norfolk, at Washington, at Brooklyn, at Charlestown, and at other places. The forts and other strongholds on the seaboard and in the interior were transferred to the new government, and positions were selected for the construction of others. Armories and arsenals for the manufacture and storage of ordnance and arms were established at Harper's Ferry, at Springfield, and at other places; and military and naval academies for the training and instruction of officers for the national service were founded at West Point and Annapolis.

In a word, all the machinery for the regular and efficient performance of those functions of government which had been committed to the central organization was arranged and put in motion without any unnecessary delay.

In the meantime, the several state governments, each within its own limits, went on in the exercise of its own reserved powers—having supreme and exclusive control over all the internal and local interests of the communities comprised within their several territories, and discharging their duties without being trammeled by any connection with the general government, still less by any dependence upon it or responsibility to it, of any kind.

The system thus inaugurated, which, though compound in its structure, is still exceedingly simple in its principles, when rightly understood, has now been in successful operation for three-quarters of a century. Under its beneficent action the country has advanced in wealth and population more rapidly than any nation of ancient or modern times; and has, moreover, been carried by it safely through two foreign wars, and has been enabled to triumph over the most formidable rebellion ever encountered by any civilized government within the period of history. We hope it is destined to endure, with such modifications as may be peacefully made in it, in accordance with its own provisions for change, till time on earth shall end.

THE END.

Lightning Source UK Ltd.
Milton Keynes UK
UKHW022224281122
413021UK00006B/140